DISTANCE EDUCATION SYMPOSIUM 3:

COURSE DESIGN

Selected Papers Presented at
The Third Distance Education Research Symposium

The Pennsylvania State University
May 1995

Edited by

Ellen D. Wagner and Margaret A. Koble

Number 14 in the series   **Research Monographs**

American Center for the Study of Distance Education
The Pennsylvania State University
403 South Allen Street, Suite 206
University Park, PA 16801-5202

The American Center for the Study of Distance Education is a collaborative effort of the College of Education and the Division of Continuing and Distance Education.

**The American Center for the
Study of Distance Education**
College of Education
The Pennsylvania State University
110 Rackley Building
University Park, PA 16802-3202

ISBN 1-877780-17-0

Table of Contents

Preface

Maintaining the Momentum

I am delighted to welcome readers to ACSDE Research Monograph No. 14, and trust that as you read the following articles, written by the leading North American researchers and thinkers about distance education, you will find much to inspire and inform you.

This monograph, Course Design, is one of a series of four, the others being Instruction, Policy and Administration, and Learners and Learning. Each monograph contains a set of articles that have been developed and edited over the past year, based on papers prepared in May 1995 for the ACSDE's Third Distance Education Research Symposium. Each monograph has been shaped and nurtured by an editor, or pair of editors, and I extend thanks to Ellen D. Wagner, Vice-President of Informania, Inc. and Margaret A. Koble, Publications Manager at ACSDE, for editing Course Design.

I have given this preface the title "Maintaining the Momentum," because I think it is important for us to remember the precedents for this particular work, to have a sense of where it is leading us, and to appreciate that what is written here is part of an on-going, indeed, historical process.

This process began in 1986 with the founding of *The American Journal of Distance Education (AJDE)*, and the establishment soon after of the American Center for the Study of Distance Education. The basic idea of the Center and purpose of *The Journal* has been to bring people together. In the United States the study of distance education, like its practice, has been highly fragmented, with little sense of community, for example, among persons researching correspondence education, education by broadcasting, and by teleconferencing. At the American Center we have tried to provide a number of vehicles for researchers, practitioners, and students who are willing to look beyond technology, who wish to identify and research the learning, instructional design, evaluation, managerial, and policy questions in distance education.

One of the first of these vehicles was the July 1988, "First American Symposium on Research in Distance Education." This was a meeting of around forty people, most of whom had shown their interest in distance education research by having an article published in *AJDE*. They were all known to the editor of *AJDE*, but not to one another. From that meeting emerged a network of persons having a better understanding of where their piece of the distance education research agenda fitted with what was going on in the rest of the field, as well as having a common sense of what needed to be done. This was the agenda for distance education research, broken down into the themes of administration and organization, learning and learner support, course design and instruction, and theory and policy.

Thirty two papers of the First American Symposium on Research in Distance Education were published in *Contemporary Issues in American Distance Education* (Moore 1990).

Following the success of the First Symposium, ACSDE used the same format in November 1990 to organize a similar event but this time focusing on the need to articulate an agenda for distance education research that was international. The first International Symposium on Distance Education Research was held in Macuto, Venezuela, prior to the 15th World Conference of The International Council for Distance Education. Again there were around fifty participants, but this time they came from a dozen countries. Once again the focus was on the state of the research and the agenda for the years ahead, though this time the question was how colleagues could collaborate internationally, not just nationally. Papers from this Symposium were published in ACSDE Research Monograph No. 5.

The impetus towards international collaboration at the Macuto symposium had one very important consequence for the evolution of distance education as a field of study and research. This was the setting up of an electronic network, known as Distance Education Online Symposium (DEOS), one of the first in distance education. By 1997, DEOS has grown to be a network of more than 4500 participants in some seventy-two countries.

A Second American Symposium on Research in Distance Education was held in May 1991, bringing together in equal numbers participants from the 1988 meeting with others who had published research in *AJDE* or DEOS during the intervening years. Sixteen states were represented as well as Canada. Participants addressed the themes: What have been the results of research since the First Symposium? What are the questions for further research? A poll of participants resulted in the following "top issues":

- Interaction of learner attributes and instructional methods
- Strategies for introducing innovations in course design/delivery
- Need for and effectiveness of interaction (faculty-student, student-student)
- Faculty/administrator development (Moore et al. 1991)

The papers of this Second Symposium were published as ACSDE Research Monograph Nos. 4, 8, and 9, limited quantities of which are available from ACSDE.

From reading these few notes, I hope it will be apparent why I said that the 1995 Symposium should be seen in its historical context. Context will show us the progress we have made, and point to the directions ahead. Just ten years ago there was no defined field of distance education research, and it has taken just ten years to reach the level of sophistication recorded in the pages of this monograph. Context also helps us understand why we are not better than we are. Our growth has been fast, and uncontrolled, and it is not surprising that some seeds, planted hurriedly and hastily brought to blossom, have not flourished. Context, provided by the papers that record the discussions at previous symposia, should help us recognize the sturdy themes, those that have been reiterated as one set of discussants has given way to another. Since each paper cites the sources of its author's thinking, we would be foolish to pass over the opportunity of identifying the pedigree underlying any question that may now appear to be of interest. These are documents that cry out to be used as a means of providing theoretical underpinning for any new venture.

So now, I invite you to turn to Ellen Wagner's introduction, and then the papers provided in this, the papers from ACSDE's Third American Symposium on Research in Distance Education. A Fourth Symposium, a pre-conference session prior to the 18th World Conference of The International Council for Distance Education, will be held at Penn State in 1997. Perhaps you will be able to refer to the themes identified in previous Symposia, and show how your research has advanced that agenda at our next symposium. If so, I will be very happy to hear from you.

Michael G. Moore

References

Moore M., ed. 1990. *Contemporary Issues in American Distance Education*. Oxford: Pergamon Press.

Moore, M., M. Thompson, P. Dirr, eds. 1991. *Report on The Second American Symposium on Research in Distance Education*. University Park, PA: The American Center for the Study of Distance Education.

1   Introduction

Ellen D. Wagner

Introduction

Course design is an essential activity associated with the study and practice of distance education. In the days when distance educators fought to have their distributed interventions considered as a viable alternative to traditional, place-bound, instructor-led experiences, course design provided a vehicle for maximizing the probability that

- the desired outcomes of a distance learning experience would be achieved, and

- the anticipated outcomes of distant instruction would be comparable to those expected in a traditional experience (notwithstanding the expectations of learners, the necessary technology mediation, and support services).

With distance education increasingly viewed as a preferred mode of instructional delivery for supporting the needs of a distributed student population, course design provides an essential strategic AND tactical element in successfully deploying distance educational initiatives.

Course Design: Two Schools of Thought

Two schools of thought appear to have influenced perceptions of course design as a conceptual entity: The practitioner's orientation toward course design represents one such school of thought and the researcher's orientation toward course design represents the other school of thought.

The Practitioner's School. In its most basic representation, a course design is nothing more—or less—than a conceptual blueprint. Its purpose is to provide parameters within which to manage all of the contingencies associated with implementing a plan to deliberately bring about a change in learning or performance. A good course design

- Identifies a learning or performance problem;

- Determines a solution for solving the problem that accommodates the context, criticality, audience, time, materials resources, or return on investment (to name just a few prospective influences);

- Defines the learning and performance objectives to be achieved for the proposed solution to succeed;

- Describes the best strategies and tactics for achieving those objectives;

- Offers a plan to ensure that key strategies and tactics are implemented appropriately; and

- Provides a framework for evaluating the value and impact of specific intervention elements on an array of course design elements.

From a practitioner's perspective, course designs provide structure for learning experiences through which behavioral, cognitive, and affective performance are likely to be improved. They offer recommendations for implementing performance improvement prescriptions in practice.

The Researcher's School. The researcher's school of thought appears to consider course design from a methodological perspective, whereby researchers treat course design as an arena of disciplined inquiry. If the discipline of course design enables the development and implementation of strategies and tactics for improving learning or performance outcomes, empirical evidence may help substantiate the theoretical constructs forming the basis of specific course design approaches. Consequently, the researcher's perspective emphasizes empirically derived measures for establishing the conceptual parameters that help define course design as a field of study.

Course design-focused disciplined inquiries tend to fall into the following three categories.

Pure Research. Pure research is conducted to establish and define an epistemological framework for the discipline of course design. From a methodological perspective, pure research can employ qualitative, quantitative, critical, historiographic, or philosophic/analytic techniques.

Applied Research. Applied research is typically conducted to determine the efficacy of specific learning and/or performance improvement techniques and prescriptions. Applied research studies help document key elements involved in various defined circumstances and assess the impact that situational and methodological variables have on those elements in controlled or observable settings.

<u>Evaluations</u>. Evaluations help facilitate better decision making by reporting on the results of course design implementations in a given setting. This information can be used to help guide the process of selecting course designs that are particularly appropriate for specific application circumstances.

Course design researchers test theories and constructs through a variety of qualitative and quantitative means. They deliberately manipulate variables to examine the impact of that manipulation on behavior or cognitive capacity. They summarize case studies, write concept papers, construct surveys and analyze data, and review professional literature of research and practice. They help define course design as both an arena of disciplined inquiry and a field of professional practice. In many respects, their efforts go a long way to legitimize course design as an intellectual discipline.

Featured Contributions to the Course Design Monograph

This monograph presents a series of papers that reflect researchers' perspectives on course design. Papers have been organized in three sections that mirror the major categories of disciplined inquiry noted above.

The first three articles relating to methodological perspectives on course design consider distance education course design from an epistemological position. In "Postmodernism, Interactive Technologies, and the Design of Distance Education," Allan C. Lauzon applies methods of critical analysis to establish a rationale for a paradigm shift regarding distance education course design. He notes that understanding the development, emergence, and application of interactive telecommunications technologies requires an understanding that technological developments themselves are a product of social, cultural, and economic forces. In his article he suggests that the emergent paradigm of constructivism may provide an epistemological framework for realizing the inherent power of distance education course designs.

Byron R. Burnham presents a systematic view of distance education and evaluation in his article, "Finding Our Bearings in Distance Education." Burnham observes that distance education has, for the past decade, been assumed to be a natural extension of existing classes, meetings, or seminars. He suggests that we consider an alternative look at distance education research and evaluation from a position that reflects the fundamental shift in practice resulting from responding specifically to the learning and performance needs of distributed learners. Burnham proposes an evaluation model/research framework that is aimed at assessing the role and impact of organization and social relationships in distance education. If these relationships were built into an evaluation or research model for distance education, then additional areas of measurement or description might be included in, or at least related to, our evaluation and research efforts.

Lynn E. Davie examines current and needed research for the advancement of practice in computer-mediated distance education course design in his paper, "Times of Turbulence and Transition in Distance Education: Needed Research in Computer-Mediated Communications." He suggests that there are four domains of research interest in the field of computer-mediated communications, and makes a case for advancing best practices in computer-mediated communications by basing course designs on research tenets arising from any one or a combination of these levels.

The second section on application directions for course design in distance education presents two papers describing the results of reviews of literature and summaries of course design applications that relate directly to specific course design practice elements. Zane L. Berge reports that computer conferencing efforts to date have either defended computer conferencing as a viable delivery system for distance education or have described the characteristics of computer conferencing and how these characteristics affect distance education efficacy. In his article, "Group Computer Conferencing: Summary of Characteristics and Implications for Future Research," he suggests that researchers turn their attention to how best to maximize benefits and minimize the limitations of computer conferencing in applied settings.

Karen L. Murphy's contribution, entitled "Designing Online Coursework Mindfully," notes that the newness of distance education cultures typically means that participants may behave in inappropriate or ineffective ways. She observes that, lacking adequate experience and training, teachers are likely to prepare online coursework without considering the impact and consequences of their behaviors on themselves, on the learners, and on the course designs they generate. Following a brief discussion of the hazards of mindlessness and the benefits of mindfulness in online coursework design, Murphy includes an overview of the characteristics of effective online coursework. The paper presents a discussion of the design of online coursework and concludes with a plea to be mindful when designing online coursework.

The last section of the monograph presents case studies in course design and development. We have the opportunity to hear three scholar/practitioners describe the results of course design initiatives with which they've been involved. In Paul M. Biner's article "Distance Learner Attitudes, Demographics and Personalities and their Relationship to College-Level Course Performance," he reports on the development of an attitudinal assessment instrument that can be used in a direct or converted fashion to monitor student reactions to their distance education courses and suggests recommendations whereby others can construct their own customized attitude instrument. He also describes profiles of successful (low-risk) and unsuccessful (high-risk) telecourse students in terms of attitudinal, demographic, and personality variables.

Cheryl Achterberg's paper, "Mixing It Up: Satellite Teaching and Hands-On Experience," describes the theoretical base for, and results of, a satellite broadcast conference for continuing education directed to nutrition practitioners working in the field. The paper presents a description of the working model used to implement the course, offers some preliminary evaluation results, and provides a discussion about the general outcomes of the experience. Dora Esthela Rodríguez describes the results of field research where students participating in the ITESM's Distance Education System reported on the quality of interactions encountered in their distance education course experiences. Her article, entitled "Interaction and the ITESM's Distance Education System," describes variables identified by students enrolled in courses transmitted via the Satellite Interactive Education System (SEIS). Since 1989 SEIS has broadcast undergraduate and master's programs courses as well as continuous education programs, with two independent transmitting channels in the Monterrey and Mexico City campuses.

Course Design: Future Directions

Ongoing technological developments and high expectations about what those technologies can offer distributed learners continue to influence the ways in which distance education course designers view their discipline. While current research continues to focus on such issues as student expectancy-achievement interactions, the role and impact of interaction in a distance educational experience, and satisfaction measures as predictors of success, we also need to investigate such issues as the dimensions of student achievement, dimensions of faculty productivity, and social dimensions of learning at a distance and factors that impact course design efficacy. Beyond these issues, even more thorny questions await our empirical considerations: Can course design methods be used to construct learning interventions that transcend the traditional boundaries of a "course"? Are we content to have traditional views of what constitutes a "course" continue to shape the direction of our "anytime, anywhere" interventions? What effect will "push" and "pull" technologies have on the expectations of individualized, distributed performance support? How will these changes affect the current model of distance education?

We offer this Monograph in the spirit of furthering the professional practice of distance education course design, and encourage readers to use these scholarly works as springboards for future considerations on defining our field of endeavor and for improving our methods of implementation.

Ellen D. Wagner

2 Postmodernism, Interactive Technologies, and the Design of Distance Education

Allan C. Lauzon

Introduction

Developments in communication technologies, particularly in the area of interactive telecommunications, have the potential for radically altering education, and in particular how we deliver distance education. Boyd (1987) suggests that computer-conferencing—one form of interactive telecommunications—is an emancipative technology, a technology that lends itself to liberative discourse and ultimately the liberation of the human spirit. Davie and Wells (1991) would seem to concur with Boyd, suggesting that telecommunication technology has the potential to liberate the distance learner. And while these authors are referring to computer-conferencing specifically, I would argue that any technology that extends opportunities for synchronous or asynchronous discourse has the potential to be emancipatory, and while claims for emancipation may seem somewhat dramatic, they are, I believe, nonetheless grounded in possibility.

Understanding the development, emergence, and application of these technologies requires that we understand that technological developments are a product of social, cultural, and economic forces. The emergence and application of a particular technology then has the potential to act on those social, cultural, and economic forces which led to their creation. These technologies then shape and mold these same forces, which then give rise to new technological developments and innovations (Boyd 1988). For example, I would argue that the development of these interactive postmodern telecommunication technologies occurred in response to the cultural evolution of industrial society into postindustrial society and movement toward an interdependent global village. However, the application of these technologies will also shape future economic and social organization and this influences the manifest form of postindustrial society. Hence, the development of these technologies is a manifestation of past and present, but also serves as a beacon illuminating changes yet to come. These technologies are a benchmark of sorts, and along with other benchmarks, are "blazing" the trail of our collective evolution, an evolution that is moving toward an increasingly complex, interdependent world, a world that demands we learn to accommodate and embrace diversity, a world in need of a more integrated and encompassing paradigm (Elgin 1993; Wilber 1995).

In this paper I propose to 1) explore briefly the dominant paradigm and distance education's relationship to that paradigm; 2) provide a brief critique of distance education as it is practiced within the context of the dominant paradigm; 3) outline the changes taking place as a consequence of a paradigm shift, and in particular examine these changes in terms of how we view knowledge, knowing, and self; 4) using Moore's (1993) three types of interaction discuss the implications the emergent conceptions of self, knowing, and knowledge have for the design of distance education; and 5) consider future steps that need to be taken, in light of the issues raised in this paper.

Distance Education and the Project of Modernity

Henderson (1981) has argued that a society's ability to solve major problems is dependent upon the dominant value system that is embraced by a particular society or culture; values are the key determinant in giving rise to the existing sociotechnical structure and paradigm. A value system is the foundation of a paradigm and is maintained by repressing modes of experience, expression and behaviors that are incongruent with the dominant values.

The dominant paradigm in the western world is one characterized by a dominator model of social organization and is expressed through scientific imperialism and colonialism. Within this paradigm there is a ranking of one-half of humanity over the other (Eisler 1987; 1991) and positivist science is viewed as the only legitimate way of knowing (Lauzon 1995). Furthermore, in North America this paradigm finds political expression in a liberal, capitalist state that values independence and self-reliance and is held together through conforming reason that dissuades the questioning of the status quo. However, this paradigm has grown dysfunctional (Capra 1982; Roszak 1989; Fox 1990), resulting in alienation (May 1953; Fromm 1976) characterized by a fragmented existence and a sense of impotency. The result has been a deterioration of the biophysical and social environment (Berry 1977; Lasch 1984; Duhl 1986). Oliver and Gershman (1989, 2) illustrate the nature of this deterioration when they write:

> It is an age in which the unconscious cultural symbols providing our lives with deep meanings are losing their vitality, the passion

that drives our love of inventing material things is drying up, and our intimate connection with the natural world is steadily decreasing. Although awed by the power of our technical achievements, we are nevertheless bewildered by the crassness that increasingly characterizes our personal relationships.

This, May (1953) has identified as the crisis of modernity, a crisis which will serve as a point of departure for our next stage of cultural evolution (Elgin 1993; Wilber 1995). The challenge presented to us by this crisis will not, however, be resolved through better techniques, changing our priorities, nor by changing our values, but it can only be met by looking at the world in new ways and redefining our relationship to it.

Inherent within this crisis is an inadequate and dysfunctional institutional structure replete with obsolete values, beliefs, and techniques. Thomas (1991) and Finger (1989) have argued that education, as an institution, evolved "indentured" to the project of modernity and consequently it is this institutional structure in which distance education finds its home, a home that is ruled by an ailing master. Birkey (1984) and Beder (1987) have argued that existing frameworks of education are designed to serve the ailing master (industrialism/capitalism) through a reductionistic stand whereby education is reduced to behavioral objectives for instilling skill and competencies. Osbourne (1982) has argued that this conceptualization of education gives rise to hegemonic conceptions of learning that contribute to the alienation of the learner. Clearly this conception corresponds with early models of distance education whereby the "challenge for the educator was to produce a perfect set of objectives, techniques, and testing devices that would fit every one of a large number of learners at a distance; no one would deviate, no one would fall between the cracks" (Moore 1994, 1). This approach was considered necessary because given the geographic distance of the student from the instructor it was the only way to control the learner. This approach to distance education is epitomized in what I would consider the mass production model of distance education. The function of the educational transaction is really designed to transmit knowledge and shape behavior—to train people to serve their master. It is here, in this approach to distance education, that behaviorism has been influential (Moore 1994), reducing education to the arrangement of contingencies that will give rise to predetermined and desirable behavior.

But behaviorism has not been the only influential philosophy that has had an impact upon distance education; the progressive thought of John Dewey has permeated the fabric of North American education, including distance education. His transactional approach to education is utilitarian and is concerned with passing on to the learner appropriate values, attitudes, knowledge, and skills. The ideal method for problem solving is the scientific method, the "only method for getting at the significance of our everyday experiences of the world in which we live" (Dewey 1938, 88). It is this scientific, utilitarian educational process that provides the state with the means to prepare responsible citizens for taking an active and productive role in a democratic society.

Also influential in distance education, particularly as it relates to the idea of the self-directed learner, is humanistic psychology with its emphasis on personal freedom, goals, and meaning (Rogers 1989). For the humanists freedom meant that the individual was responsible for seeing oneself clearly and taking responsibility for one's life situation; the individual was responsible for choosing and acting in his/her own best interest. Maslow (1970, 179) echoes these sentiments when he argues that education is to assist the learner with determining "what is good and bad, knowing what is desirable and undesirable, learning what to choose and what not to choose," while acknowledging that the learner is ultimately the one in charge of learning.

This educational perspective has clearly influenced distance education. For example, Moore (1994, 1) suggests that the educational transaction be characterized by a more open partnership between learners and instructor, with learners assuming an active role in the identification of goals, means, and evaluation methods. This, he argues, is valuable and desirable and that "designers of what we would now call distance education programs should take into account these abilities." Clearly humanistic psychology and its educational expression through principles of adult education has influenced the practice of distance education.

Distance Education and the Project of Modernity: A Critical View

When I read the distance education literature I often ask myself if we have viewed our own work with a critical eye. I am afraid I usually answer no. Recognition of the need for lifelong education has given us a new found status, a status that recognizes that distance education has a central role to play in enhancing the quality of life of people around the world; now I wonder if we are so enamored with the attention we are finally receiving from our ailing master that we are only too eager to please him. I am afraid conforming reason has prevailed, and we have failed, as a community, to look critically at what we do and the assumptions we make. Schumacher (1977, 55) once wrote: "Every thing can be directly seen except the eye through which we see. Every thought can be scrutinized except the thought by which we scrutinize."

Schumacher is correct, and it is only through critical reason that our paradigm and value system can be truly examined and challenged. Our time has come, it is time to challenge our paradigm and our assumptions. This, however, can be a difficult and painstaking process for it questions all that we do and are.

First, the above discussion characterizes the foundations on which distance education has been built, a foundation which has been influenced by many different sources: the behaviorism of B. F. Skinner, the progressive thought of John Dewey, and humanistic psychology as characterized by the writing of Carl Rogers and Abraham Maslow; it truly is built upon an eclectic foundation. And while some argue this is a strength, I believe it is a weakness. An eclectic approach begins by borrowing from a multiplicity of sources, sources that begin with different assumptions; hence, it is not possible for an eclectic foundation to find expression in a unified vision. Collins (1991) argues that this leads to an education characterized by a technocratic ethos which is driven by the invisible hand of the marketplace, leaving education an impotent player.

Second, the paradigm in which distance education is embedded, as influenced by behaviorist, progressive, and humanistic thought, is founded upon androcentric and ethnocentric presuppositions that have been constructed by economic and chauvinist values that exclude women and other minority concerns (Lauzon 1995; Paringer 1990). hooks (1994) argues that although education has been viewed as a means of realizing one's freedom, it has become distorted and perpetuates racism, sexism, and imperialism. Bell and Schniedewind (1989) maintain that while humanistic assumptions have contributed to our understanding of how individuals change, the implicit assumptions made about the apolitical, decontextualized self mean that we have failed to examine structural differences in power, institutional discrimination, and historical antecedents. Failure to do this often results in the further marginalization of marginalized people.

Burstow (1994) argues that the apolitical, decontextualized self is problematic as freedom is premised on the myth of the "self made man" and the "American Dream," and this denies that we exist as beings-in-relation; freedom requires that we recognize our relationships and responsibilities to others. Burstow (1994, 6) further argues that embodied in the self of self-directed are "alienated males' values and modes of operating singularly valued and turned into method." This is evident when we ask students to set their own goals and determine their own learning activities, but then insist that they establish valid and objective evaluation criteria, collect adequate data, and provide evidence for the purpose of evaluating the learning outcomes. While we give learners freedom to choose we still wish to ensure that they use valid methods and criteria, methods and criteria that reflect alienated male values. Clearly this does not support what Belenkey et al. (1986) call "connected teaching," teaching that honors beings-in-relation. The problem is further exacerbated when we try to use "connected methods" and use words like dialogue, co-learner, etc. and then encourage learners to view their peers as a human resource to be accessed to assist in their studies; this objectifies people and perpetuates the exploitation of others.

Furthermore, when we do attempt to involve people in truly learning together, we take a simplistic approach and have a tendency to psychologize our analysis. For example, Moore (1994) attributes group success or failure to individual personalities within the group and absolves the "instructional designer" of any responsibility for success or failure. This analysis fails to recognize that hierarchical structures and defined roles tend to recapitulate themselves in all social organization—including learning groups. Moore has failed to consider power relations, who is in the group, what are group members perceptions/experiences, etc. He simply assumes that it is a matter of individual personalities or learners not being sufficiently autonomous to function in a group. And while these issues are a problem, Burstow (1994) argues that they are simply symptoms of a larger problem: the uncritical acceptance of elite males' modes of operating and behavior being used as the standard for exemplary adult behavior.

As educators, our jobs should be in working for the liberation of the human spirit, all human spirit and this, I believe, requires that we bring a critical analysis to our own educational practice and a critical analysis of the institutions we work in. For without social critique and consciousness-raising, the "self in self direction is more fictitious than real" (Burstow 1994, 8).

An Emerging Paradigm: A Constructivist Perspective

Allender (1987) has argued that the monolithic structure that I called the dominant (positivist) paradigm has been undermined by 1) Kuhn's work on the structure of scientific revolutions, demonstrating the consensual basis of all scientific activity, and 2) Polyani's argument that we need to recognize the inherent connection between our personal subjectivity and any attempts to be objective. Furthermore, Polanyi introduced the importance of tacit knowing as a legitimate way of knowing within the context of scientific inquiry (Allender 1987).

The starting point in the postmodern journey requires that we acknowledge that our distinctly human experience is mediated by symbols, and it is through symbols that meaning is derived. This, as Ogilvy (1992, 47) reminds us, is "always culturally and linguistically tinged and therefore never entirely innocent." If we accept this premise then it must follow that knowing is culturally conditioned and hence normative. The myth of a world out there waiting to be discovered cannot be known separate from the system of symbols that we use for knowing (Allen 1989). Thus, knowledge is constructed and not discovered.

One of the dangers of this perspective, according to Varela (1989), is that all knowing is influenced by an aggregate of the subjective and historical and, therefore, we are not ground in any stable reference point. Thus, knowing is not only shaped by culture but will also be shaped by individual ontogenies. This has led Guba and Lincoln (1989) to describe constructivism as a heuristic, subjectivist epistemology whereby the inquired and the inquired-into are interlocked and the findings of the inquiry process are a creation of the process of inquiry.

Acceptance that knowledge is shaped by culture and personal ontogeny then means that the fact/value dichotomy, characteristic of traditional approaches to constructing knowledge, must be transcended, for any question asked of "reality" will have either an explicit or implicit value dimension (Allender 1987). According to Guba and Lincoln (1989), all facts are value-laden and have no meaning independent of the value framework in which they are situated. Therefore, all knowledge created within a particular value framework will be situation specific and localized.

Thus, the constructivist's approaches to knowing is characterized by a relativist ontology whereby any number of socially constructed realities, ungoverned by any natural causal laws, may exist at one time (Guba and Lincoln 1989; Smith 1994). Cause and effect do not make sense within the context of a constructivist paradigm, and we can only understand reality as the interaction of a number of shapers, each acting and responding to other shapers. This then raises the question as to how we come to a common understanding of what is real. The answer is that the construction of knowledge is a social process whereby the sharing of experience and constructions widens our understanding of the phenomenal world and this process of sharing occurs through dialogue. Guba and Lincoln (1989) describe this methodology as hermeneutic, and it is characterized by a continuing dialectic of iteration, analysis, critique, reiteration, reanalysis, etc., leading to a shared understanding of some aspect of the phenomenal world. Truth is realized when there is consensus about the constructions used to represent reality.

Inherent within the context of the constructivist paradigm is the idea that all knowledge, and the process of knowing itself, is a political act; knowledge fused with values, culture, and personal ontogeny is explicitly political and has implications for existing future relationships and social organization. Thus, the idea of the self is a social construction and hence a cultural artifact infused with values (Cushman 1990). The self of the traditional paradigm is constructed as isolated, self-reliant and apolitical, and this construction is empty, naive, and inadequate (Sampson 1989; Cushman 1990; Hermans, Kempen, and van Loon 1992). No longer is the "atomization" of self adequate for understanding the social world or meeting the demands of an increasingly interdependent world. In fact, individualism is antithetical to cooperative interdependence. The emergent view of self is best described as constitutive whereby a person's attachments to community are constituents of their identity. After all, it is these attachments which shape the individuals' knowing and constructions. Thus, according to Hermans, Kempen, and van Loon (1992), personal identity within a constitutive perspective then becomes a process of personal narrative that recognizes that identity is based upon a multiplicity of dialogically interacting selves.

Inherent within this conceptualization of knowledge and self is recognition that power is implicit within relationships and language. This is noted by Sampson

(1993, 1222) when he writes "categorization is discursively constructed presumably with the dominant groups interests in mind." Therefore, "power involves the manner by which persons are given a location and a subjectivity as actors within discourse." He concludes by stating that as long as marginalized groups use the voice of those who have constructed them, they continue to be complicit in their own domination. Clearly, within the context of the traditional paradigm, distance learners have been requested to subjugate themselves to one way of looking at the world and, willingly or unwillingly, have been complicit in their own domination. We, too, as educators who have subscribed to this paradigm, have been guilty in engaging in a process that fosters oppression. Liberation lies in finding and developing educational processes that allow for diversity and recognize that knowledge is constructed, that it is built by people dialoguing in community, learning to name the world for themselves.

Designing Distance Education from a Constructivist Perspective

The emergence of the constructivist paradigm challenges us to think critically about learning and how we can design distance education to meet the needs of the constructivist knower. One starting point is to take Moore's (1993) three types of interaction—learner-content, learner-instructor, learner-learner—and examine them from a constructivist perspective.

Learner-Content Interaction. This interaction is the interaction that is necessary, according to Moore (1993, 20), for without it education would not be possible; it is the process of intellectually interacting with content that results in "changes in the learner's understanding, the learner's perspective, or the cognitive structures of the learner's mind" that constitutes an educational outcome. It is the mastery of the content that usually determines an educational transaction as successful.

This conceptualization of the learner-content interaction from a constructivist perspective proves somewhat problematic. Traditionally content is viewed as universal and objective. A constructivist, however, would argue that "objective" content is simply one construction and would likely claim that it represents a privileged perspective. They would also argue that it only has validity within the context in which it was constructed. Its application across contexts is not valid from the constructivist's perspective. Furthermore, attempts to argue that it is a "generalizable truth" is oppressive to those who were not involved in its construction. What function then can this "objective" body of knowledge serve?

First, if we acknowledge that it is one construction, we can use it to invite students into a process of dialogue with the theorists/author(s), other students, or with ourselves. If the material is appropriate we can ask students how it fits with their experience. Often when learners are invited to do this, they find elements of the construction are useful in understanding their own experiences: they find labels for raw experience which then allows them to explore the internal dynamics of their own experience systematically and learn to name the world (Griffin 1987).

Now, that is all fine and well if learners are engaged in study that is directly related to human experience, but what happens when learners are studying biology or chemistry? How can they relate that to their own experience? The answer to this question is they probably cannot. But we can invite learners into understanding how the various theories or perspectives were constructed: for example, understanding the historical and cultural context in which a theory was generated or studying biography and understanding what it was that motivated the individual and where his/her passion came from. When we approach "objective knowledge" from this perspective, we soon learn that in fact it is not objective, and not abstract, but it is tied very intimately with a specific historical and cultural context and may have been given a certain flavor because of the subjective experience of an individual. Learners can be asked to examine how times are different and what the implications are for the theory. Through doing this learners begin to see the interconnections, that knowledge cannot be understood independent of values, culture, biography, and action.

Thus, the pedagogical function of the learner-content interaction is to provide an entry point for inviting the learner into a process of dialogue with self and perhaps history, and to learn to see how human understanding evolves and changes.

Learner-Instructor Interaction. Moore (1993) describes this interaction as an interaction between the student and the expert, who in addition to instructing will attempt to motivate. In describing the dynamic of this interaction, Moore (1993, 21) articulates the responsibilities of the instructor as: 1) making presentations or making students do presentations, 2) organizing the material to be learned, and 3) organizing evaluation to determine the learners' progress.

From the constructivist perspective this is clearly an abuse of power whereby the learner is requested to subjugate his knowledge and experience to the expertise of the instructor. While it can be acknowledged that the instructor may have a more informed construction than the learner, it is a construction nonetheless. Instructors should help learners understand the intricacies of the construction as discussed above and invite students to enter into a dialogue with the construction and those who have made it. It is also an opportunity for the instructor to enter into authentic relationship with the learner and share her or his own understanding of the construction, thoughts and feelings, etc. Often within the context of traditional approaches to education we are asked to give a balanced view of the field and this may mean presenting ideas which we personally oppose intellectually, emotionally, or ethically. We need to share our insights and beliefs with our learners and in doing this we breathe life into abstractions. Opportunities then arise to enter into relationship as co-creators of knowledge with learners, and this shifts the balance of power whereby they too can teach us through the sharing and exploration of constructions together.

Moore also suggests that the instructor is responsible for motivating the learner, but there is no greater motivator then to enter into authentic relationship and to explore ideas, not as isolated and removed abstractions, but as messy existential realities where actions, values, and beliefs are all mixed in together. Kegan (1982) states that what makes us human, what differentiates us from other animals, is our need for meaning. The process of education should be meaningful and the instructor has an opportunity to invite the learner into a process for creating personal meaning.

The pedagogical function of the instructor then is to assist learners in understanding the intricacies of the construction and to help learners bring their own experience into dialogue with the construction. Also, the instructor should enter into the process of dialogue with the learner and share his or her insights and beliefs, recognizing that by doing so he/she invites the student into the dialogue process through authentic relationship. Once relationship is established the instructor can help the learner begin to explore the constructs in terms of relevance to the learner's own history and experience. This, in itself, is motivating for the learner.

Learner-Learner Interaction. The last interaction Moore (1993) identifies is the learner-learner interaction. He argues that this interaction is dependent upon the circumstances of the learners, their age, experience, and level of autonomy. It is interesting to note, however, that often educators "value" student-student interaction but are not always sure of its pedagogical purpose, particularly in the absence of any learner expertise.

From a constructivist perspective this interaction is essential. Knowing (learning) is a social act that requires that learners enter into a dialogue with others, to share stories out of which we build constructions. The feminist concept of consciousness raising is an excellent example where learners share their stories and out of the stories they collectively learn to construct and name their world. This, in essence, happens in community. Here, in community, learners have a safe environment in which to share stories, to take risks. And in creating a safe community we provide an opportunity for conflict to be worked through, for a constructivist approach to knowledge is filled with conflict as we iterate, analyze, critique, reiterate, reanalyze, etc. our realities. Thus, by entering into dialogue, we build communities that allow us to exist in-relation-to-others in our learning. And it is only when we learn-in-relation that we truly come to know.

Thus, the pedagogical function of the learner-learner interaction is to create a safe environment for learners to explore, risk, and name their world and at the same time challenge others, and together construct knowledge.

Self-Self Interaction. I believe that Moore (1993) has missed one interaction, one that I believe is essential to all real knowing and that is the self-self interaction. By this I mean simply our capacity to reflect on our knowing and reflect on how we come to know, which can be described as meta-knowing.

First, our ability to reflect on how we know, or on our meta-knowing, is essential for personal growth and development. It is this motion, the evolution of meaning making, that Kegan (1982) identifies as the primary movement in personality. Thus, it is only on reflecting on how we know that we move toward the realization of our potential.

Second, the self-self interaction also provides opportunities that allow the learner to begin to integrate emergent constructions into his or her personal paradigm. The traditional approach to learning believed in a knowledge that was discovered outside of us, in the material world. Hence, when we learn it requires that we take something into us from the outside world. A constructivist perspective would argue that this is not possible, that learning is the very process through which the world is brought forth. Learning does not happen from "out-in", but emerges from "in-out." We cannot deny our subjectivity and must acknowledge that ontology will influence the world we bring forth. Our whole personal history will influence how we construct knowledge and the types of constructions we create and how we integrate them into our existing personal paradigm. Thus, within the educational transaction there needs to be a space provided where self meets self and the learner reflects on the worlds he or she has brought forth, and the worlds that they will continue to bring forth. It is this self, a self that exists in-relation-to-others and exits in-relation-to-self, that brings forth the world that is shared, yet unique for each individual.

Thus, the pedagogical function of the self-self interaction is simply to create a space to reflect on one's knowing in order to derive meaning from our knowing by reflecting on that which we have brought forth, and to reflect on the very process by which we bring the world forth. It is this interaction that provides opportunities for deriving meaning from our knowing, facilitating our development and forcing the redefining of our relationship to the world.

The Next Step

As I sit here and reflect on what I have written and its implications for future research, I realize that I cannot identify any neat and tidy research projects that need to be done. We exist, in the words of William Irwin Thompson, on the edge of history. What is needed is a serious dialogue among distance educators as to what distance education should be; we need to create a vision. Our new-found status makes this imperative. And in creating this vision we need to delineate the role of telecommunications within the context of distance education and new emerging concepts of knowledge, knowing, and self. Boyd (1987) offered the opinion that the new telecommunication technologies can be emancipating, but he also cautioned that they can be domesticating. Traditional approaches to learning, have, to a certain extent, used educational technologies to domesticate through encouraging and rewarding conforming reason. Our job as educators has been to socialize learners into a way of looking at the world, a way that is alienated. If we perpetuate this vision of education, we will use the new telecommunications technology to assist the "master" in extending his technocratic grip. We do not have to serve him or follow his path; we can embark on creating our own path as distance educators. Tomorrow offers not only a new day, but a new world if we choose it to be. We can choose to follow or we can choose to lead. If we choose to lead, then critical moral discourse is a necessity. I hope you will join me in that discourse.

Conclusion

This paper began by talking about interactive technologies, yet I have said little about them. I have not discussed bandwidth, compression, speed, capacity, or any other technical "stuff." I am not enamored with hardware. I look at the interactive telecommunication technologies, and I see opportunity, opportunity for people to reach out across vast geographical spaces to embrace one another, to engage in dialogue, and to bring forth a new world that is truly a global village. I have spent a great deal of time talking about the constructivist perspective, but in talking about it I have really talked about the technologies too, for they are a manifestation of the same forces that are giving rise to new conceptions of knowledge, knowing, and self. As distance educators we sit upon a precipice overlooking what could be. A new world waits below us if we can find the courage to take the steps and leave behind that which we have known, that which has become arid, that which no longer nourishes life. I hope we have the courage to take that step.

In drawing this paper to a conclusion I would like to leave you with a few questions to think about.

- As distance education programs become increasingly international, how do we accommodate different cultures and values in the distance learning community?
- How can we, as researchers and practitioners of distance education, help others make the transition from an education designed to serve industrialism to a distance education that is designed to serve the postindustrial order?
- What technical and interpersonal skills will learners need to participate in the postindustrial distance learning community?
- As a practicing distance educator, how do my values and beliefs inform or hinder my educational practice?

- How should distance education be organized to ensure accessibility to all who desire or need access to it?
- How will the development of distance education be different in the postindustrial era than in the industrial era?
- How can distance education best help to meet the collective challenges we face?

These questions represent a sampling of what we, as distance educators, must begin to consider, contemplate, and answer, recognizing that our answers will have a direct impact on how we design distance education and enter into relationship with learners.

Note: For the purpose of this paper I will use the phrase interactive technologies to refer specifically to the postmodern telecommunication technologies that allow us to readily communicate with others either synchronously or asynchronously, and that permit multi-patterns of communication. This would include such technologies as computer, audio and video conferencing as stand alone technologies or as elements of integrated multi-media systems.

References

Allen, P. M. 1989. Toward a new science of human systems. *International Social Science Journal* 119:81–91.

Allender, J. S. 1987. The evolution of research methods for the study of human experience. *Journal of Humanistic Psychology* 27(4):458–484.

Beder, H. 1987. Dominant paradigms, adult education, and social justice. *Adult Education Quarterly* 37(2):105–113.

Belenkey, M. F., B. M. Clinchy, N. R. Goldberger, and J. Tarule. 1986. *Women's Ways of Knowing: The Development of Self, Voice and Mind*. New York: Basic Books.

Bell, L., and N. Schniedewind. 1989. Realizing the potential of humanistic education: A reconstructed pedagogy for personal and social change. *Journal of Humanistic Psychology* 29(2):200–223.

Berry, W. 1977. *The Unsettling of America: Culture and Agriculture*. San Francisco: Sierra Club Books.

Birkey, C. J. M. 1984. Future directions for adult education and adult educators. *Journal of Teacher Education* 35(3):25–29.

Boyd, G. 1987. Emancipative educational technology. *Canadian Journal of Educational Communications* 16(2):167–172.

Boyd, G. 1988. The impact of society on educational technology. *British Journal of Educational Technology* 19(2):114–122.

Burstow, B. 1994. Problematizing adult education: A feminist perspective. *Canadian Journal for the Study of Adult Education* 8(1):1–14.

Capra, F. 1982. *The Turning Point: Science, Society and the Rising Culture.* New York: Simon and Schuster.

Collins, M. 1991. *Adult Education as Vocation: A Critical Role for the Adult Educator.* New York: Routledge.

Cushman, P. 1990. Why the self is empty: Toward a historically situated psychology. *American Psychologist* 45(5):599–611.

Davie, L. E., and R. Wells. 1991. Empowering the learner through computer-mediated communication. *The American Journal of Distance Education* 5(1):15–23.

Dewey, J. 1938. *Experience and Education.* New York: Collier Books.

Duhl, L. J. 1986. Health and the inner and outer sky. *Journal of Humanistic Psychology* 26(3):46–61.

Eisler, R. 1987. *The Chalice and the Blade.* San Francisco: Harper Collins.

Eisler, R. 1991. Technology, gender, and history: Toward a nonlinear model of social evolution. *World Futures* 32:207–225.

Elgin, D. 1993. *Awakening Earth: Exploring the Evolution of Human Culture and Consciousness.* New York: William Morrow and Company.

Finger, M. 1989. New social movements and their implications for adult education. *Adult Education Quarterly* 40(1):15–22.

Fox, M. 1990. *A Spirituality Named Compassion.* San Francisco: Harper San Francisco.

Fromm, E. 1976. *To Have or To Be?* Bantam Books.

Griffin, V. 1987. Naming the process. In *Appreciating Adults Learning, from the Learner's Perspective,* eds. V. Griffin and D. Boud. London: Kogan Page.

Guba, E. G., and Y. S. Lincoln. 1989. *Fourth Generation Evaluation.* Beverly Hills, CA: Sage Publications.

Henderson, H. 1981. *The Politics of the Solar Age: Alternatives to Economics.* Garden City, NY: Anchor Press/Doubleday.

Hermans, H. J. M., H. J. G. Kempen, and R. J. P. van Loon. 1992. The dialogical self: Beyond individualism and rationalism. *American Psychologist* 47(1):22–33.

hooks, b. 1994. *Teaching to Transgress: Education as the Practice of Freedom.* New York: Routledge.

Kegan, R. 1982. *The Evolving Self: Problems and Process in Human Development.* Cambridge, MA: Harvard University Press.

Lasch, C. 1984. *The Minimal Self: Psychic Survival in Troubled Times.* New York: W.W. Norton & Company.

Lauzon, A. C. 1995. Exploring the foundations of an adult education for a sustainable culture: The unfolding story continues. Unpublished manuscript.

Maslow, A. 1970. *Motivation and Personality* (2nd edition). New York: Harper and Row.

May, R. 1953. *Man's Search for Himself.* New York: W.W. Norton and Company.

Moore, M. 1993. Three types of interaction. In *Distance Education: New Perspectives*, eds. K. Harry, M. John and D. Keegan. London: Routledge.

Moore, M. 1994. Autonomy and interdependence. *The American Journal of Distance Education* 8(2):1–5.

Ogilvy, J. 1992. Future studies and the human sciences. *Futures Research Quarterly* Summer:5–65.

Oliver, D. W., and K. W. Gershman. 1989. *Toward a Process Theory of Teaching and Learning.* Albany: State University of New York Press.

Osbourne, J. W. 1982. The hegemony of natural scientific conceptions of learning. *American Psychologist* 37:330–332.

Paringer, W. A. 1990. *John Dewey and the Paradox of Liberal Reform.* Albany: University of New York State Press.

Rogers, C. D. 1989. *The Carl Rogers Reader.* Boston: Houghton Mifflin.

Roszak, T. 1989. *Where the Wasteland Ends: Politics and Transcendence in Postindustrial Society.* Berkeley, CA: Celestial Arts.

Sampson, E. E. 1989. The challenge of change for psychology: Globalization and psychology's theory of the person. *American Psychologist* 44(6):914–921.

Sampson, E. E. 1993. Identity politics: Challenges to psychology's understanding. *American Psychologist* 48(12):1190–1230.

Schumacher, E. F. 1977. *A Guide for the Perplexed.* New York: Harper and Row.

Smith, B. M. 1994. Human science—really! A theme for the future of psychology. *Journal of Humanistic Psychology* 34(3):111–116.

Thomas, A. M. 1991. *Beyond Education: A New Perspective on Society's Management of Learning.* San Francisco: Jossey-Bass.

Varela, F. S. 1989. Reflections on the circulation of concepts between a biology of cognition and systemic family therapy. *Family Process* 28:15–24.

Wilber, K. 1995. *Sex, Ecology, Spirituality: The Spirit of Evolution.* Boston: Shambhala Publications.

3   Finding Our Bearings in Distance Education: A Systemic View of Distance Education and Evaluation

Byron R. Burnham

Introduction

Distance education is a growing and developing field in a number of regards. First, it is growing in the numbers of people participating; second, it is growing in the numbers of sponsoring organizations; third, it is growing in the diversity of sponsoring organizations; fourth, it is developing in its sophistication of programs; and fifth, it is developing in sophistication of methods. Distance education methods vary from learning approaches which are tutorial-like with basically one-on-one interaction to large mass-audience endeavors which can literally involve tens of thousands of people in almost unlimited locations.

To accompany these areas of growth and development, a correlative area of conceptual and theoretical thought must be developed. Out of necessity, due mainly to rapid growth, "research in distance education has been dominated by attempts to answer questions of immediate, practical significance" (Scholosser and Anderson 1994, 16). For a number of years the idea that distance education was mostly a natural extension of existing classes, meetings, or seminars, with learners who were separated from the instructor in either time, or distance or both, guided our activities in distance education research and evaluation. This paper suggests an alternative look at distance education research and evaluation, and proposes an evaluation model/research framework built upon that alternative view.

That distance education should be recognized essentially as a different kind of endeavor from traditional face-to-face education has been recognized by those working and writing in the field and in other closely related areas. For example, Garrison (1989) offers three criteria as minimum characteristics of a distance education setting. He notes that in distance education a majority of educational communication occurs noncontiguously, two-way communication between teacher and student occurs, and communication is technologically mediated. These criteria or elements differ from another view best represented by Holmberg (1986) wherein he emphasizes the isolated nature of distance education. Garrison's criteria better represent a North American view with its emphasis on technologically mediated communication. A common element shared by both positions is that the teacher and learner are separated in either time or space or both.

These characteristics described by Garrison are provided by a distance educator and reflect the field-view of distance education. Closely related to this definition is that of the American Association for the Advancement of Science's definition of technology (1989, 39): "In the broadest sense, technology extends our ability to change the world: to cut, shape, or put together; to move things from one place to another; to reach farther with our hands, voices, and senses."

While various authors writing in the field of distance education and those writing in closely allied fields find common or related perspectives, there remains a problem with those who look at distance education with only technology in mind. This fact is lamented by Hofmeister, Carnine, and Clark (1993, 2) when they say that

> Many of the present conceptual structures surrounding technology, media, and materials are hardware-focused and detract from more potent variables, such as the content and structure of the curriculum, the supporting pedagogy, and the interaction between the teacher and the technology, media, and materials. The electro-mechanical components provide the needed vehicular or dissemination role.... We diminish the values of and the focus on this dissemination role when hardware is promoted with questionable claims implying unique and powerful contributions to the learning process.

These problems can be greatly reduced if the phenomenon of distance education is conceptually viewed in a holistic manner. It is the purpose of this paper to present one such view.

A Framework for Understanding

The following framework is presented in some detail so that its implications for evaluation and research and building related frameworks can be readily identified. While the original framework is over thirty years old, its conceptual underpinnings are current and can serve distance education researchers and evaluators well because they are based on timeless concepts which undergrid much modern research in the social sciences.

In the early 1960s Coolie Verner proposed a conceptual scheme for classifying various components of adult education transactions. He did this because he felt that "the generally recognized confusion that characterized adult education stems from the absence of any conceptual scheme or basic theoretical structure" (Verner 1962, iii). While Verner wrote about adult education, his arguments apply equally well to the broad field of education and to the narrower sub-field of distance education. Verner's framework depends upon the precise use of two popularly confused terms: methods and techniques. To Verner they meant vastly different things and those differences can and should inform our practice of distance education.

Verner (1962, 9) defined method as "the relationship established by the institution with a potential body of participants for the purpose of systematically diffusing knowledge among a prescribed but not necessarily fully identified public." This idea of method is limited to organizational and sociological concerns. It does not encompass the psychological construct of learning (Mark 1994). While much effort has been directed toward learning in our studies of distance education, little has been aimed at the organization and social relationships in distance education. If these relationships were built into an evaluation or research model for distance education, then additional areas of measurement or description might be included in, or at least related to, our evaluation and research efforts.

Technique was defined by Verner (1962, 9) as "the relationship established by the institutional agent to facilitate learning among a particular and precisely defined body of participants in a specific situation." Verner's notion was that methods refer to ways in which organizations relate to groups of people and techniques refer to the ways in which people relate to information for the purpose of learning. Techniques are exemplified by lectures, role-plays, group discussions and other *learning* techniques. Techniques deal with learning transactions. Relative to methods this is the area in which much research and evaluation has taken place. But it should be noted that Miller (1994, 211) says, "in the United States...discussions of distance education often tend to be dominated by technology, administrative and students support issues. In such an environment, distance educators tend to perceive curriculum as an issue over which they have little direct control."

Methods, according to Verner, provide us with a set of techniques appropriate to given situations. Methods can be individual in nature, such as apprenticeships, correspondence study, or internships. Group methods can be classified into natural groups (such as a family or autonomous groups) or social groups (such as formal associations or work groups). Small groups, larger groups, and community groups are all possible classifications. Methods and techniques are related then as to how well one (methods) can accommodate the other (techniques).

Verner understood the place of technology hardware or, as he labeled them, "devices." This notion of devices is particularly informative and places a new light on what we term technology. Verner (1992, 10) stated:

In producing educational activities for adults, numerous mechanical instruments or environmental factors may be employed to augment the processes employed. These are frequently identified by the field as methods or techniques when in reality they should be designated more precisely as <u>devices</u>, since they enhance the effectiveness and utility of a technique but cannot themselves function independently as techniques for the acquisition of knowledge.

Verner (1962, 13) also understood that any method of education was the function of the "continuing relationship for systematic learning that is established by the institution with those in the public whom it seeks to educate...." Then, according to this description of method, individual needs and institutional needs combine to determine the method. Verner implies in his writings that some techniques are method bound. Certainly, an instructional designer would not employ a group discussion technique in a method in which learners exist in isolation (i.e., an apprenticeship). Once methods and techniques have been selected, then devices can be chosen, because devices, in and of themselves, do not teach. This linear approach to instructional design has also influenced evaluation and research models, most of which begin with goals and objectives (or hypotheses), then consider ways to determine to what extent those goals or objectives have been met. This traditional approach to both instructional design and evaluation does not fit modern distance education as the updated framework presented below demonstrates.

An Updated Framework

The flow of the traditional instructional design process is from method to technique to device and is well exemplified by Dick and Cary's (1978) systematic approach to instructional design. Verner in the early 1960s could not anticipate the advent of the smart devices which exist today. Burnham and Seamons (1987, 10) proposed "the idea that devices, especially electronic devices and systems, can affect methods or even create methods unanticipated by Verner...." These new methods have not received much attention from researchers in distance education. We have been so caught-up with demonstrating that there are no statistical differences between distance education and face-to-face educational outcomes that we have forgotten the notion that we are dealing with another kind of educational setting or method which may very well call for a new paradigm of evaluation and research, or which at the very least will affect the traditional lock-step notion of instructional development.

To illustrate the differences, consider for a moment the traditional classroom method of education where students are assigned to a class or register for one. While it is true that the student composition of the university class today is more diverse than in the past, it is also true that the student composition of distance education classes is even more diverse. Consider for a moment the kinds of students that may be in the same distance education class: displaced homemakers, unemployed space industry workers, and inmates from the state prison. How do these people interact with one another? Another and more fundamental question is, What constitutes a classroom or learning group? Is it the total of the people at the various sites or is it the total at each receiving site? As Miller (1994, 216) noted "Our technology allows us to create new kinds of learning communities." Verner would have labeled these methods. It is important to realize that the classroom method is changed by the new devices we encounter in distance education. We are mistakenly attributing learning affects to the devices when we might be better advised to consider the effects of methods and techniques which are enabled or disabled by devices.

This is precisely the point made in the *Blueprint for Action* (Hofmeister, Carnine, and Clark 1993). The advantage of using the labels with specific references to particular areas of education means that differentiation can be made among technology (the devices), the organization for distance education (the methods), and instructional design matters or processes for facilitating learning (the techniques). Such differentiation will help avoid the problems noted by Burnham and Seamons (1987) as they described a metaphor of distance education: "The current landscape of Electronic Distance Education (EDE) is broken and confused by boulders of hardware, rivers of processes, and mountains of exhortations.... Because of technological changes and improvements, the future seems encumbered with even more conceptual confusion and technological preoccupations than is presently the case" (Burnham and Seamons 1987, 8). The comments of the American Association for the Advancement of Science 2061 project staff would indicate that the statement was prophetic to some small degree.

A distance education system can be simply represented by Figure 1, wherein the relationship of devices, methods, techniques, learners, content, and instructors are portrayed in relationship to one another. The solid lines which encircle the instructor and content represent the fact that instructors possess some information about the subject matter being taught and learned. In Figure 1 the term "instructor" could be replaced with the term "institution" to make it more congruent with Verner's framework. Instruction is used here to indicate a broader view of the educational transaction than limiting it to an institutionally based enterprise, which Verner's approach may tend to do. It is interesting to speculate about the degree to which learners have independence when they rely upon devices which are rather complex and are institutionally controlled or managed. This is another example of how devices affect the transaction between learners and instructors and among learners themselves.

The gap between the instructor and learner is the physical separation of, or the dialogue/structural distance between, the instructor and learner. The gap between the learner and content represents the lack of information, skills, or attributes which is the focus of the learning event. While it is acknowledged that learners do possess life experiences that may involve the content being studied, they do not necessarily possess the degree of information or

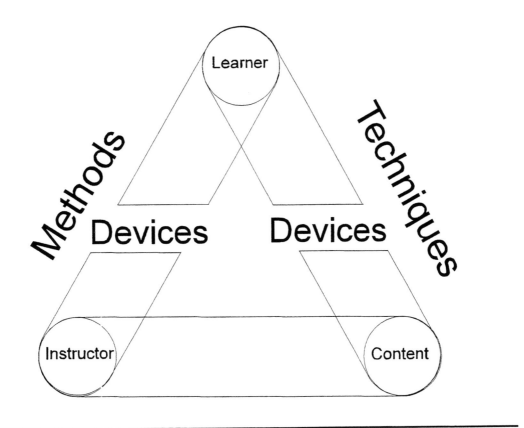

Figure 1. An Electronic Distance Education System

perspectives represented by the instructor. Both gaps, between the instructor and the learner and between the content and learner, point to the isolation of the learner. In distance education these gaps are bridged with devices which are sophisticated and alluring, sometimes to the point of seducing evaluators and researchers into focusing on them as the sole object of study. Methods and techniques are enabled and created by the bridging devices. These objects and constructs could profitably be the evaluation objects or research study constructs.

This conceptual framework can be used to develop a research framework or an evaluation model for distance education. Such a framework allows researchers and evaluators to understand not only which part of distance education they are studying but also what categories of the teaching-learning process (method, techniques, or devices) are involved. Thus it helps avoid confusing distance education organization and instruction into some amorphous mass of related activities that are treated similarly. The framework or model can also help direct investigators into methodological considerations as well as measurement concerns. The model presented in Figure 2 is built upon the concepts from Figure 1. Concepts which formed the framework in Figure 1 are transformed into areas for evaluation in Figure 2. Some concepts such as "content" in Figure 1 make little or no sense as an area for evaluation or research (unless we want to determine subject matter appropriateness for distance education). What remains in the model are the instructor, the learner, devices and, not so obviously, methods and techniques.

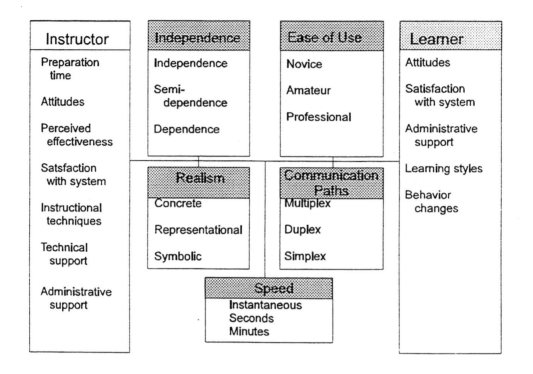

Figure 2. An Evaluation/Research Model for Distance Education

Methods and techniques are explored from the perspectives of the instructor and learner when questions about effectiveness and satisfaction are asked. Evaluation and research methods for effectiveness might well involve experimental or quasi-experimental approaches. There is a growing body of literature which deals with various techniques and their effectiveness in various settings and with various audiences. Because distance education is growing and diversifying at a rapid rate, evaluation and research studies related to the methods, techniques, and devices employed in distance education become critical to both theory and practice.

Devices are represented in Figure 2 by five characteristics which are inherent in a given device and contribute to a distance education setting. The characteristics were originally present by Stubbs and Burnham (1990). Those device characteristics include: ease of use, communications paths, speed, realism, and independence. As mentioned earlier the independence of learners may be a function of who controls or manages the learning device. These device characteristics allow or enable the creation of new methods and techniques beyond those defined by Verner. But more importantly these characteristics move devices beyond the rather passive role which Verner described for them, to a more active role in which they define and modify the very environment in which distance education occurs.

The other two elements of Figure 2 represent the learner and the instructor where perceptions of each can be examined in regard to several areas. For example, instructors have ideas, feelings, or thoughts about the number of hours they spend in preparation for distance education classes. Learners also have perspectives about attitudes, support, learning, and other learner related areas.

This framework or model provides help in understanding how various evaluation or research efforts in distance education may or may not relate to one another. For example, issues of satisfaction with the system, administrative support, personal learning styles, behavioral changes, and the like can be studied from the learners' perspectives or within the contexts of methods, techniques, and devices. Learners can provide perspectives on the learning environment (both methods and techniques) that can guide instructor behavior. This framework has been used to guide a number of research and evaluation endeavors in distance education. One of the more intriguing studies involved observing distance education receiving sites in an audioconferencing program. Parallel learning, one finding from that study, is used here to illustrate how implications from evaluation and research efforts can be considered within the framework described above. This finding has implications for instructional design (techniques), distance education administration (methods), and technology (devices). To better illustrate these implications a brief description of parallel learning is offered here.

Parallel learning describes that activity in which adult distant education students engage whenever instruction slows or becomes irrelevant or whenever some other event occurs which affects an "instructional stream." Distance education provides a setting where adults appropriately can and do talk to one another about what is being discussed. And during these discussions they process information that is relevant to the topic at hand.

We have found from observing distance education at remote sites that students do not sit passively awaiting instruction from all-knowing experts. To the contrary we found adults actually guessing what the expert was going to say next, or debating what had been said. They interacted with the instructor but they interacted more frequently and longer with fellow students at the local site. This interaction produced insights which participants indicated would change their behavior—that is to say, learning had taken place.

Figure 3 illustrates what might be called the instructional stream, which is largely under the direction of the instructor. However, there are events which encourage distance education students to engage in the behavior of parallel learning. There are other episodes which cannot be classified as parallel learning, which are actually non-parallel in nature. The trigger events may be a disruption in the signal to the remote site, an especially boring lecture, unusually controversial statements by the instructor, irrelevant statements, etc. Less well documented are those events which return the learners to the instructional stream.

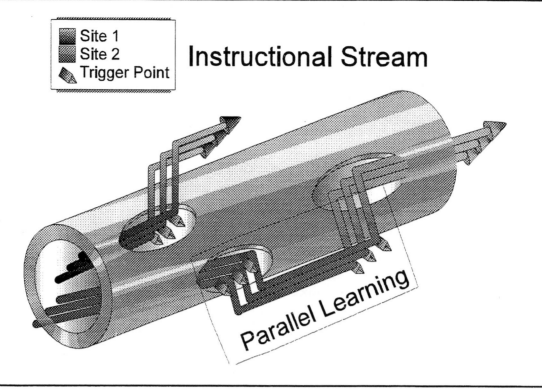

Figure 3. The Instructional Stream

The implications for the instructional designer are to help teachers manage trigger events by avoiding them and to maximize their effect when appropriate (employment of proper techniques). For the technology system manager implications have to do with the smooth running of a system (devices). And for the distance education administrator implications are for the socialization of learners to a distance education system (methods).

I am concerned that instructional development will in the future be concerned with message design, graphics, public speaking, and instructor mannerisms and will neglect the part of information dissemination that turns an activity into education (methods, techniques, and devices). When you think about it, satellite distance education is not much different from watching television unless attention is given to methods, techniques, and devices. Methods, techniques, and devices are all elements that interact much more than previous researchers and theoreticians have suspected. We need to study these elements, including the relationships, so as to better understand the dynamic enterprise called distance education.

Conclusion

In conclusion, it seems fitting to address the important questions posed by the organizers of the Third Distance Education Research Symposium. I will do this based on the points raised in my paper and upon some experiences I have had as a practitioner of distance education.

Question: What is research showing us about quality in distance education? Quality often is a function of the student, not of the learning situation. Research into the National Endowment for the Humanities (NEH) funded distance education programs show that instructors find students learn at faster rates than campus-bound students. Students in both learning situations end at about the same place, but the distance education students have further to travel on their learning journeys. When one considers the fact that distance education students are likely to be adults, then we must ask the question about our measures and just what they are measuring. Perhaps we may be confusing the nature of the learner with the circumstance in which they learn. I am not sure distance education research tells us much about the quality of learning.

Question: What is missing in the research about good quality in distance education? One of my points whenever I speak or present is to talk about the lack of information about student behavior at the remote site. We know little about it. I have heard students say their distance education experience was boring and that it was a good thing the teacher could not see them, because they were not on task, or not even in the room.

Question: What recommendations can be made to improve the quality of research in distance education? We need more participant observational studies. We need more descriptions of behavior and what that behavior means to the actor. We need more theoretical approaches to the study of distance education. We too often trip over the technology in our attempts to study the phenomenon of learning at a distance.

These questions and answers are from only one perspective. When we as a group of researchers share findings, discuss problems, and inspire and support one another, other answers, better answers will surely come to us.

References

American Association for the Advancement of Science. 1989. *Science for All Americans*. Washington, DC: American Association for the Advancement of Science.

Burnham, B. R., and R. A. Seamons. 1987. Exploring the landscape of electronic distance education. *Lifelong Learning: An Omnibus of Practice and Research* 11(2):8–11.

Dick, W., and L. Carey. 1978. *The Systematic Design of Instruction*. Glenview, TX: Scott, Foresman.

Garrison, D. R. 1989. Distance education. In *Handbook of Adult and Continuing Education*, eds. S. B. Merriam and P. M. Cunningham, 221–232. San Francisco: Jossey-Bass.

Hofmeister, A., D. Carnine, and R. Clark. 1993. A blueprint for action: Technology, media, and materials. Working paper. Washington, DC: American Association for the Advancement of Science.

Holmberg, B. 1986. *Growth and Structure of Distance Education.* London: Routledge.

Mark, M. 1994. The differentiation of institutional structures. In *Contemporary Issues in American Distance Education*, ed. M. G. Moore, 11–21. Oxford: Pergamon Press.

Miller, G. E. 1994. Distance education and the curriculum: Dredging a new mainstream. In *Contemporary Issues in American Distance Education*, ed. M. G. Moore, 211–220. Oxford: Pergamon Press.

Scholosser, C., and M. Anderson. 1994. *Distance Education: Review of the Literature.* Ames, IA: Research Institute for Studies in Education.

Stubbs, S. T., and B. R. Burnham. 1990. An instrument for evaluating the potential effectiveness of electronic distance education systems. *The American Journal of Distance Education* 4(3):25–37.

Verner, C. 1962. *A Conceptual Scheme for the Identification and Classification of Processes.* Washington, DC: Adult Education Association of the USA.

4 Times of Turbulence and Transition in Distance Education: Needed Research in Computer-Mediated Communication (CMC) Course Design

Lynn E. Davie

Introduction

This paper is intended to examine current and needed research for the advancement of practice in computer-mediated distance education course design. While there is a wide variety of ways in which distance teaching and learning designs can be mediated using computers, the particular focus of this paper is on the use of computer-mediated conferencing software specifically designed to facilitate communication among learners and instructors.

These are times of great transition in the technical resources available to distance education designers. With transition, turbulence is not uncommon. In the past ten years, most computer-mediated distance education has used computer conferencing software for designs where individuals participated in distance education courses from home or work. In the past two years, connections to the Internet have grown immensely and important new developments such as the graphical browsers for use with the World Wide Web (WWW) have made the Internet even more accessible. The newest designs will take advantage of the integration of the WWW software with computer conferencing for asynchronous learning settings. This paper, therefore, will focus on computer conferencing distance designs and will look at the integration of computer conferencing programs with Internet tools.

Contextual Model

To situate current research, I propose the following model of computer-mediated distance education. There are four domains of interest. First, and most basic, are the physical technologies and basic software protocols. The second domain categorizes major computer applications programs which are useful for organizing teaching and learning. The third domain focuses on educational designs from the point of view of the instructors or institutions. Finally, the fourth domain centers on learning designs from the point of view of individuals or groups of learners. Advancements of practice may be based on research in any one of these levels.

The First Domain: Physical Technologies and Basic Software Protocols. Although this paper will not focus on the physical domain, it is important to note that many of the changes to the practice of computer-mediated distance education are made possible by the rapid growth in both the capacities of computers available to learners and the ways in which these computers are interconnected. The average computer purchased in 1995 is a multi-media machine with a fast processor, massive amounts of memory and storage, and the ability to handle both sound and video. These machines can be, and often are, connected to networks of vast breadth and depth. Collectively known as the Internet, these networks allow for the storage and transmission of large quantities of information, including text, sound, graphics, and full motion video. The basic software of the Internet, such as ftp, telnet, e-mail, gopher, and the WWW allow easy access to the most remote outpost on the Internet. While the use of these machines, networks, and programs for educational purposes has just begun, the growth is accelerating at a rapid rate. Having a clearer understanding of the fit between educational needs and physical technologies may help identify interesting educational research in this domain.

The Second Domain: Application Programs. This domain contains the major application programs that support the organized educational use of computers. Major computer conferencing programs, such as FirstClass, Participate, CoSy, as well as mail list programs such as listserv and majordomo are examples. Primary improvements in computer conferencing programs in recent years have been on user interfaces. With the more powerful graphical capabilities of individual computers, easier to use graphical user interfaces for most of the computer conferencing software have been developed. Based on client-server technology, local machines with a variety of platforms (i.e., Macintosh, DOS, Windows) can interact with servers located on mainframe computers.

In addition, there have been important developments in software used to access the Internet. In the past year, a major development has been the development of Mosaic, a browser for WWW pages. This fairly simple to use graphical program interprets data (text, graphics, sound, or video) and displays these data in attractive ways with little intervention or technical knowledge required of individual users. In the past few months, a competitive program known as Netscape has become available and within six months has over 6 million users, and there are many commercial products in the design stage. The availability of these programs has spurred growth on the Internet in geometric proportions.

The Third Domain: Educational Designs from the Instructor's or Institution's Point of View. Research and theoretical work in this domain focuses on the effectiveness of instructional designs. Here is located the research into constructivist cognitive learning, cooperative learning designs, and the investigations into appropriate knowledge structure and portrayal. Concepts such as tele-apprenticeship, hyper-media portrayal of information, or cooperative work can be examined. Some of these concepts will be addressed in greater detail later in the paper.

The Fourth Domain: Learning Designs from the Individual Learner's or Groups of Learners' Point of View. This final domain addresses research and theory that help us understand the learning transaction from the viewpoint of the learner. Issues of motivation, information overload, and learning style are the foci of investigation in this domain. While there is an important overlap between the educational and learning designs, they remain distinct categories of research. This domain will be highlighted in the sections that follow.

Review of Research

The amount and variety of current research in each of the four domains is vast. In this paper, I plan to review past and current research at The Ontario Institute for Studies in Education (OISE). Though a small institution, some significant doctoral research is being conducted in the latter two domains.

Since OISE is an educational graduate school and research institution there is no current research in the physical technologies or applications programs domains. Although our computer applications faculty are currently working on integrating computer conferencing programs with WWW pages, this work is in its earliest stages and has not been published. In the educational designs and learning designs sections, completed work as well as a short description of a number of doctoral research projects in progress are included.

The Third Domain: Educational Designs from the Instructor's or Institution's Point of View. There are two time relationships among participants in computer conferencing. In the synchronous model the participants are online at the same time and converse in a kind of real time. Conferences on large on-line services such as Compuserve, America Online, or Prodigy would be examples of synchronous conferencing, as well as the Internet Relay Chat (IRC) programs on the Internet. The other major model of conferencing is asynchronous where participants are not online at the same time. Most computer conferencing systems use an asynchronous model, such as electronic mail lists, Participate, CoSy, or FirstClass.

Two of our doctoral graduates, Wilton (1987) and Higgins (1992), were interested in investigating the effects of the time relationship among students.

Their theses have investigated the effects of synchronous vs. asynchronous conferencing. Wilton (1987) studied a group activity involving forty-two students (aged 15-17) in use of a synchronous computer conference on a local area network. She found that synchronous networked software was successful in supporting a group problem-solving task, and that participants found communication through the network adequate for task performance as well as personally satisfying.

Higgins (1992) studied "the comparative effects of synchronous text-based CMC with asynchronous text-based CMC in terms of cognitive and cooperative activity, the quality of outcome and subjective impressions of the participants." Higgins found that the synchronous mode was more effective in key cognitive activities such as "managing the task," "problem formulation," and "interactive arguing." The synchronous dyads also exchanged more cooperative and facilitative remarks. Finally, ratings of the student output were higher for the synchronous dyads (Higgins 1992, i).

Winkelmans (1988), in a M.A. thesis, demonstrated a number of relationships among notes in an educational CMC conference. His work clearly mapped the effects of instructor contributions on subsequent conference notes.

McKinnon (1993) studied 139 distance students enrolled in the same grade-12 distance education course, Introduction of Law. Three experimental groups were formed. Group A was made up of volunteers who took the course by CMC. Group B was composed of students randomly assigned who used regular mail to take the course. Group C was also composed of randomly assigned students who took the course by regular mail, but they also had telephone contact with the instructor to negotiate a learning contract. Six measures were collected: start-up rate, completion rate, completion time, lesson average mark, final examination mark, and final course mark. There were no differences in the measure of completion rates between Group B and C, the randomly assigned regular mail groups. However, on all other measures Group C, with the telephone contact, had better results. Group A, the volunteer CMC group, had even better results, although comparison is difficult since this final group had not been randomly selected.

Cairns (1994) studied the facilitation process in computer conferencing courses. She interviewed twelve experienced distance education teachers who use CMC in six different institutions. From a qualitative analysis of these respondents, Cairns described a facilitation process that includes: 1) the creation of a safe intimate community for learning; 2) the teachers' awareness of the learning capabilities of the adult learner; and 3) a variety of teaching roles. She said, "Computer conferencing enabled the teachers to implement a style of pedagogy which reflected the implementation of individualized instruction, self-directed learning and student-directed learning" (p. i).

Finally, Chandler-Crichlow (1994) studied the effect of facilitators' use of cognitive intervention strategies on cognitive performance of learners involved in computer mediated conferences. By systematically varying the kind of summary notes (simple summary vs. synthetic summary) written by facilitators, she was able to demonstrate that cognitive performance is related to the intervention role of the facilitators.

Currently four theses are underway studying various phenomena of CMC education from the point of view of the facilitator or course designer. Each thesis deals with a generic educational issue or design. Mary Anne Andrusyszyn is investigating the effects of including reflective activities in CMC educational designs. She has arranged for a number of CMC instructors to include journaling and other reflective activities in their courses and is studying student reports of learning. Preliminary results were reported in a conference paper (Andrusyszyn and Davie 1995).

Susan Cole is working on examining the use of collaborative metaphors in the notes of online courses. She is looking at the development of a communal meaning among students who work together. A thesis by Don Robertson also focuses on the changing use of language over the duration of a CMC course. He is investigating the relationship of language use to effectiveness in participation and the way in which vocabulary changes. These theses, taken together, should provide a better understanding of the development of shared meanings and common language over time.

Finally, Judy Norris is examining the use of electronic-based apprenticeships to facilitate the transfer of knowledge from experts to students. Her expert/student pairs communicate through an electronic mail list with the apprentices sharing their thoughts through online journals and the experts providing support and commentary. Issues of support, challenge, and effectiveness are being examined.

The Fourth Domain: Learning Designs from the Individual Learner's or Group of Learners' Point of View. While the theses in the previous section have implications for learning from the learners' point of view, Burge (1993, 1994) paid particular attention to an in-depth qualitative investigation of students' perceptions of learning in computer conferencing. She found that participants identified a set of learning strategies and a set of learning conditions, based on identified strengths, weaknesses, and features of the CMC contexts. The students' learning strategies focused primarily on the cognitive domain, with the major categories being choice, expression, group interaction, and the organization of information. The conditions for learning focused upon relational, affective, logistical, and cognitive elements.

Needed Research

This final section highlights research that might prove useful for improving the practice of CMC education. Due to the limits of space, no attempt will be made to suggest research in the domain of physical technologies and basic software protocols other than to say that, at this basic level, improvements in network access, storage, and display devices and better user interfaces are perennial needs. In addition, current research in virtual reality is quite promising for synchronous CMC education applications.

The Second Domain: Application Programs. A significant problem identified by CMC students is the feeling of information overload. This problem is probably very complex including issues of cognitive psychology, real information loads, and lack of skills in managing information. One possible line of research to this problem might lie in the development of intelligent software agents. Current development of intelligent software agents have provided early prototypes which can help manage your electronic mailbox, search for information on the Internet, or search commercial databases. You instruct these software agents with preferences, and they filter and arrange information in ways that best conform to your style (Horberg 1995).

Nicholas Negroponte (1995, 155) described the concept of intelligent agent in terms of human analogies:

> In fact, the concept of "agent" embodied in humans helping humans is often one where expertise is indeed mixed with knowledge of you. A good travel agent blends knowledge about hotels and restaurants with knowledge about you (which often is culled from what you thought about other hotels and restaurants). A real estate agent builds a model of you from a succession of houses that fit your taste with varying degrees of success.

I think there is a major opportunity for the development of software that could be thought of as a personal tutor. You might begin by training your agent in your preferred learning styles and preferences for the arrangement of information presented to you. In addition, the agent would watch your learning activities and make changes in your preference profile based on your actual learning behaviors. Included as a part of the agent would be the search engines being developed for searching the various protocols of the Internet, such as gopher servers, libraries, and the WWW. You begin by instructing Tutor Agent about what you want to learn. It engages you in a dialogue to clarify your request, goes out to the Internet and finds information that meets your specification. The Tutor Agent then organizes and presents the found information in ways that best meet your learning styles and preferences. We can even imagine our Tutor Agent negotiating on your behalf with a university to assign credit to your learning.

The Third Domain: Educational Designs from the Instructor's or Institution's Point of View. In looking at needed research from the Instructor's point of view, it is helpful to look at two of the many roles that an instructor plays.

Instructional designer. This role involves choosing the content of the course, arranging it in meaningful ways, setting the requirements and assignments, and structuring the learning environment. Needed research to support this role might include continuing research in structuring and portraying knowledge (i.e., continuing studies of the effectiveness of hypertext and multi-media), or research into effective assignment structures which would encourage social construction of knowledge. Studying the differences of learning environments created by different software designs (such as the difference between graphical and text based browsers for the WWW or gopher sites) would have merit. In addition, perhaps there is room for exploring the utility of mentorship of the new CMC instructor in the development of expertise with the concepts of instructional design and delivery.

Counselor. The role of counselor is to assist the learner with trouble-shooting the problems involved in learning. The counselor performs the role of psychological or emotional support for the course. Students may be isolated in their community, at least in terms of having someone with whom to work out the frustrations commonly associated with taking courses by CMC or other means. Students often express the need for someone to whom they can express themselves without reservation. The counselor can provide needed support and encouragement to help learners overcome hurdles and maximize opportunities for success and satisfaction. While services can be provided in face-to-face settings, we need to investigate the counseling and support services needed by on-line students and experiment with different ways of organizing and providing needed services.

The Fourth Domain: Learning Designs from the Individual Learner's or Group of Learners' Point of View. Probably the most pressing problem in CMC education from the learner's point of view has to do with the overwhelming array of information now available. The problem of information overload was discussed above in terms of providing of intelligent software agents. However, this problem could benefit from a number of research approaches. For example, is the feeling of information overload related to inexperience in taking courses this way? Could institutions provide computer courses that help students learn how to study in this medium (Kuffner 1984)?

Another area of needed research is in the development of learner empowerment. We have argued elsewhere (Davie and Wells 1991) that empowerment is composed of two elements: a sense of competence and a sense of community. We need to investigate what skills are related to a feeling of competence in computer-mediated communication. Since no one can know all there is to know, there must be a threshold of perceived skill for each person that allows her/him to operate at minimal levels of stress in the CMC learning environment. Similarly, we need to know how to facilitate the sense of community. There are many anecdotal reports of strong feelings of community as well as reports of sensed isolation. What makes the difference? Is it an individual characteristic, or are there elements of the CMC environment that either make it more welcoming or hostile?

These investigations will take place in a rapidly evolving on-line communication space. December (1995, 5) argued,

> Unlike the 1970s dreams of on-line media as conduits for "products" delivered to consumers (Hiltz & Turoff, 1978), the reality of the

1990s involves more complex interactions, many of which take place for non-economic reasons. This growing diversity in how people use on-line communication challenges those studying CMC.

Finally, we tend to think of CMC education as institutionally based, an extension of the classroom. But what of possible research into the person on the street and the possible learning relationships with the agencies and organizations involved in providing services to that person—from garage mechanics to social workers? How does or will CMC be used in informal settings as a learning tool? We might explore how service providers via the Internet are being used by individual learners. How do they find the resource they need? How do they use the resource? What would they like to see different? How do they identify their own needs?

Summary

This paper has reviewed some of the research being conducted at The Ontario Institute for Studies in Education and suggested a number of directions for research that could provide insight into the ways that important meaningful learning can be encouraged. Needed research has been suggested into variables of import from both the instructors' and students' points of view.

References

Andrusyszyn, M. A., and L. E. Davie. 1995. Reflection as a design tool in computer mediated communication. In *Distance Education Conference Proceedings*, ed. L. Dooley. San Antonio: Texas A & M University.

Burge, E. J. 1993. Students' perceptions of learning in computer conferencing: A qualitative analysis. Unpublished Ed.D. dissertation. Ontario Institute for Studies in Education, University of Toronto, Toronto, Ontario.

Burge, E. J. 1994. Learning in computer conference contexts: The learners' perspective. *Journal of Distance Education* 9(1):19–43.

Cairns, Beth J. Sleightholm. 1994. The facilitation process in computer conferencing courses: The perspectives of teachers. Unpublished Ed.D. dissertation. Ontario Institute for Studies in Education, University of Toronto, Toronto, Ontario.

Chandler-Crichlow, C. 1994. A comparison of facilitators' use of summarizing vs. synthesizing intervention techniques on cognitive performance in computer mediated conferences. Unpublished Ph.D. dissertation. Ontario Institute for Studies in Education, University of Toronto, Toronto, Ontario.

Davie, L. E., and R. Wells. 1991. Empowering the learner through computer-mediated communication. *The American Journal of Distance Education* 5(1):15–23.

December, J. 1995. Transitions in studying computer-mediated communication. *Computer-Mediated Communication Magazine* 2(1), January 1, 1995. [Online] Uniform Resource Locator http://www.rpi.edu/~decemj/cmc/mag/archive.html.

Higgins, R. N. 1992. Computer-mediated cooperative learning: Synchronous and asynchronous communication between students learning nursing diagnosis. Unpublished Ph.D. dissertation. Ontario Institute for Studies in Education, University of Toronto, Toronto, Ontario.

Hiltz, S. R., and M. Turoff. 1978. *The Network Nation: Human Communication via the Computer*. Reading, MA: Addison-Wesley Publishing.

Horberg, J. 1995. Talk to my agent: Software agents in virtual reality. *Computer-Mediated Communication Magazine* 2(2), February 1, 1995, p. 3. [Online] Uniform Resource Locator http://www.rpi.edu/~decemj/cmc/mag/archive.html.

Kuffner, H. 1984. Computer-assisted applications in distance teaching and evaluation. *Distance Education* 5(1):38–49.

McKinnon, N. C. 1993. An assessment of using technology and learning contracts with adult learners in distance education. Unpublished Ed. D. dissertation. Ontario Institute for Studies in Education, University of Toronto, Toronto, Ontario.

Negroponte, N. 1995. *Being Digital*. New York: Alfred A. Knopf.

Wilton, J. A. 1987. User behaviour in synchronous computer networked learning environments. Unpublished Ed.D. dissertation. Ontario Institute for Studies in Education, University of Toronto, Toronto, Ontario.

Winkelmans, T. 1988. Educational computer conferencing: An application of analysis methodologies to a structured small group activity. Unpublished M.A. thesis. Ontario Institute for Studies in Education, University of Toronto, Toronto, Ontario.

| 5 | **Group Computer Conferencing: Summary of Characteristics and Implications for Future Research** |

Zane L. Berge

Introduction

The union of telecommunication technologies and computer networks have given us new tools to support teaching and learning. Taken together, these tools can be used for *computer-mediated communication* (CMC). Santoro (1995) lists three categories of CMC: computer conferencing, informatics, and computer-assisted instruction. Within computer conferencing, Santoro (1995) identifies three types: electronic mail (e-mail), group conferencing systems, and interactive messaging systems. The aim of most designers of computer conferencing environments is "not merely to duplicate the characteristics and effectiveness of the face-to-face class. Rather we can use the powers of the computer to actually do better than what normally occurs in the face-to-face class" (Turoff 1995).

The case for computer conferencing as a viable means for teaching and learning in distance education has been documented by Hiltz and Turoff over the past two decades (Turoff 1995) and by many others more recently (see Bellman 1992; Berge and Collins 1995a, 1995b, 1995c; Harasim 1990a; Hiltz 1994; Mason 1990; Mason 1993a; Mason and Kaye 1989; Wells 1992). It should be emphasized that computer conferencing does not have to be the only channel for delivery of instruction. In fact, the integration of computer conferencing into the overall course and program is an exciting, yet relatively unexplored area of inquiry.

The characteristics and "advantages" of computer conferencing (CC), which appear in Table 1, have also been exhaustively described (see, Beaudoin 1995; Bellman 1992; Berge and Collins 1995a, 1995b, 1995c; Harasim 1990; Hiltz 1994; Lehman et al. 1993; Mason 1990, 1993a; Mason and Kaye 1989; Wells 1993). I consider these characteristics, for example asynchronous communication, to be *neutral* with regard to the teaching/learning process. For instance, the fact that group computer conferencing can be characterized as providing an environment that is text-based and thus being "low in social context cues," compared with face-to-face interaction, can have both negative and positive consequences in an instructional setting. Low levels of social context cues appear to set the stage for more uninhibited behavior on the part of computer conferencing users in some virtual venues than would occur face-to-face (Sproull and Keisler 1991; Sudweeks and Rafaeli 1996). This can lead to rapidly escalating misunderstandings and violent arguments, but it can also facilitate more interpersonal interaction in a class setting and involve persons who are normally shy or wary in a face-to-face classroom (Bellman 1992). And so it is with each of the characteristics of group computer conferencing listed in Table 1.

Instructional designers usually hold an implicit and personal compilation of theories about what teaching and learning should look like. Certain roles and functions of the CC participants are assumed by a designer in order to turn the characteristics of computer conferencing to educational uses. The designer must first know what those characteristics of the instructor(s) and learners are and what impact the assumptions about their roles and functions may have on the teaching and learning situation, which itself is in a state of constant change along many different dimensions.

Further, it appears that reports on the design of computer conferencing to date have mostly been of two types: first, authors (mostly practitioners) have defended computer conferencing as a viable delivery system for distance education; secondly, authors/researchers have described the characteristics of computer conferencing, and how these characteristics are advantageous in distance education. My conclusion is that researchers need to turn their attention to the conditions under which each advantage operates and how best to maximize benefits and minimize the limitations of computer conferencing.

In this paper I will summarize the characteristics and advantages of group computer conferencing systems and discuss limitations. Following that, I will mention some of the myriad assumptions and changing dimensions of our curriculum, teaching techniques, students and teachers roles, the technological environment, and the institutions that sanction teaching and learning through CMC.

Group Computer Conferencing. Group conferencing computer programs range from simple e-mail exploders (e.g., Listserv) to sophisticated bulletin-board systems (e.g., Usenet News), through conference management systems (e.g., VAXnotes) and on to Group Decision Support and Electronic Meeting Systems

Table 1. Characteristics of Group Computer Conferencing with Corresponding Advantages for Teaching and Learning

Characteristics	Advantages
Asychronous Communication	• time independence permits 24 hour access to other people and resources • may be more convenient for student meeting work, family, and other responsibilities • self-paced learning; allows time to compose responses
Synchronous Communication	• course documents(s) can be modified by more than one person simultaneously • real-time discussion and brainstorming • shares some flexibility with spoken word • (NOTE: designers of distance education should note that this characteristic cancels the advantages of time independence)
Provides a virtual space for social networking, changing roles, and dimensions of students, teachers, curriculum, and institution	• facilitates course management (e.g., advising, organizing materials, collecting/returning assignments) • role of student as more life-long, independent, learner-centered; student takes more responsibility for learning • interdisciplinary, multiple perspective approaches; permits work on messy, but authentic, problem solving • role of teacher as facilitator and collaborator • supports group, collaborative/cooperative activities • students and teachers become part of a virtual community of learners; multi-cultural; international • opens doors to planned events (personal networking) and to unplanned interactions (serendipity)–both course and non-course related; professional development • allows mentoring and apprenticeship models to be used between faculty and students • allows sensitivity to learner's preferences and style • allows for peer review of projects and peer learning
Provides a technological environment combining telecommunication systems and computer networks to solve problems of access, quality, and productivity	• place independence • text-based • has relatively low social context cues • often fosters less inhibited behavior • possibly a more egalitarian classroom atmosphere where a contribution is judged by the content not the author's appearance or characteristics • archiving of course content, posted assignment or other information germane to class; student missing class can use archives • provides practice using technological tools which may be useful in all course work/job market • provides access to the world's people and resources • relatively fast communication channel

(Turoff 1995). All varieties of computer conferencing share some or all of the following asynchronous and synchronous characteristics:

- A directory for identifying participants and addresses on the system
- Electronic mail
- Conferences for group discussions, with a permanent record of interactions
- Private work spaces for collecting ideas
- Word processing for drafting or revising documents, perhaps by multiple users simultaneously
- Bulletin boards for access to announcements
- Newsletter or journal for access to articles or papers
- Databases for access to information, files, and documents
- Voting or polling for determining support for an issue

When all the above features are combined, as in groupware, a very powerful environment for computer-supported cooperative work in classroom/laboratory settings is formed (Sweet, Anderson, and Halenda 1991) Perhaps with the exception of synchronous communication these features are likewise beneficial in distance education.

Generally, researchers in the field have identified certain aspects of group computer conferencing as providing advantages for instructional design (Romiszowski and de Haas 1989; Mason 1991; Berge and Collins 1993; Turoff 1995). These computer conferencing characteristics are: communication that is either synchronous or asynchronous (but usually asynchronous); communication that is text-based and carries a relatively low level of social context cues; and an environment that is a virtual space for social interaction via a combination of computers, telecommunication systems, and computer networks. With few exceptions (e.g., Sproull and Kiesler 1991), authors identify a set of advantages, often doing so by comparing courses delivered face-to-face or in a "traditional" classroom setting approach to similar courses delivered at a distance.

Characteristics and Advantages of Group Computer Conferencing

Asynchronous Communication. Computer conferences can be conducted using some form of basic mail handling software, like listserv, listproc, and majordomo. The mailer program is given a list of all participants in the "conference." Participants use the e-mail facilities of their home computers to compose, send, receive, and read contributions to the ongoing discussion, which may or may not be moderated or facilitated. Messages arrive in a sequential stream as they are posted and are not organized into topics or "threads"—thus Santoro (1995) classifies this as a "one-to-many" type of conference. For the most part, the organization of these messages is the responsibility of the receiver, and for a new user, this can be a confusing task (Morrison 1993; Romiszowski and de Haas 1989). Some mailer software can create archives, usually on a weekly or monthly basis depending on the amount of traffic, and copies of this compilation can usually be electronically requested by conference participants.

Another format for computer conferencing involves students actually logging into a specific location, which may or may not be at their home institution. The conference program is designed to provide a teaching and learning environment constructed in software and available via the Internet (Turoff 1995). The conference program holds all the messages, and displays them on multiple "bulletin boards" that may be called "branches," "conferences," "topics," or "rooms." Messages can be read sequentially or in "threads" using the subject line or the "branch" or "conference name" as a guide. Responses to messages can be posted to the appropriate thread and left for other readers. With messages stored in a central location, this is very efficient for distributing messages, but receipt depends on conference users logging in to a central location to read them. This can limit the use of the computer conference to those who have the facility to telnet to other locations. Conferencing software like VAXnotes or CoSy belong in this category of "many-to-many" communication.

In asynchronous communication, because the central computer supporting the computer conference usually operates twenty-four hours a day and seven days a week, users can work at a time that is convenient to them and fits in with their personal schedules. It is frequently not necessary for all group members on a project or in a class to be in the same place at the same time for face-to-face meetings, nor online for virtual meetings, provided the conference is frequently checked for new messages.

Before participants respond to postings, they can take time to reflect and consider their response (Fowler and Wheeler 1995; Vygotsky 1962), and they can accumulate data and references with which to substantiate their arguments and positions. This permissible time-lag in computer conferencing is particularly well suited to shy, thoughtful, or hesitant conversationalists and to members of those cultures (for instance, Native American) where answers and responses are to be considered and carefully framed before presentation (Baldwin 1995). Under face-to-face conversational circumstances their hesitation can cause problems, as the lack of immediate response may be taken to indicate that a response will not be forthcoming. Fast-thinking speakers may continue in their conversational turns and slow responders will lose theirs. In CC a response time lag of hours or even days may be acceptable with the only consideration being the norms developed within the group regarding permissible response time lags. Respondents who are eager to participate can respond to messages as soon as they read them, and they may make multiple contributions. Group norms usually arise concerning the number and frequency of postings.

Learning becomes more self-paced in this environment (Hiltz 1994). (Of course, along with "self-paced" comes the responsibility of the students to be self-motivated in their work habits.) This can be extended to break down the idea of fixed semesters and course schedules, although it is better in practice to have all conference members present from the beginning of the course, as it takes a "critical mass" of participants to sustain discussion (Romiszowski and de Haas 1989).

Synchronous Communication. Computer Conferencing is a tool that promotes "many-to-many" communication. The conference environment is a place where students can interact among themselves and with their instructors almost as if in a face-to-face setting (Bellman 1992; Rawson 1990). Through such interaction, it is possible that content can be formulated and reformulated, and with each assimilation and reconstruction, the learner's understanding can grow. Not only is task oriented discussion facilitated, but also the social interactions (Schrum 1993) that are part and parcel to most face-to-face instruction.

When students need feedback that is novel or needed quickly, the synchronous (or near synchronous) aspect of CC becomes useful. With real-time group discussion, students can brainstorm ideas or, given the appropriate computer conferencing system (i.e., groupware), students can modify a common document. However, synchronous communication is problematical in many respects in distance education. Most notably, since people have to all be online simultaneously, synchronous communication negates time independence, one of the many advantages that distance education offers.

Provides a Virtual Space for Social Networking, Changing Roles, and Dimensions. An essential technological element in computer conferencing, as opposed to listserv managed groups, is that all users must have the software, hardware, and telecommunication capabilities to use a common computer where the computer conference program resides. Given this, separate areas can be set up in some computer conferencing programs as common work areas for use by small, collaborative workgroups, or they can be accessed by the entire group. Discussion areas, functioning like individual bulletin boards, can also be set up by topic. A contribution by a "guest lecturer" (Cotlar and Shimabukuro 1995) could be posted to such a topic-specific bulletin board area, read by those logging in, and then copied or saved to individuals' private work areas. Commentary on the guest lecture could then be posted for others to read. For classroom assignments, this can take on the flavor of peer review and peer learning where appropriate.

The term "salon" has come to refer to short-duration computer-mediated conference groups associated with face-to-face professional conferences where several papers may be archived prior to the conference. Salon subscribers can retrieve and read them and then comment on or discuss the papers, often with the authors' participation. This not only gives conference attendees a voice in ways that may not be possible during formal, face-to-face sessions, but many persons who can only "virtually" attend can also participate. Student access to this kind of activity allows them to watch scholarly debate as it occurs, and they can observe and learn in the manner of a cognitive apprenticeship (Collins 1991; Collins, Brown, and Newman 1989).

One type of general area that is often set up in classroom conferences is a "commons" or "cafe" where conference members can electronically meet and greet one another, and where the conversation is social rather than task related. This takes the "chat" to a specific area for students to interact and build community, but allows task-oriented individuals to continue working undistracted. For some persons it is all they can do to log on and read the task-oriented material, and they tend to react strongly to what they consider frivolous or time-wasting chatter (Collins and Berge 1994). As in many communities, the support for a more student-centered, interactive learning process requires careful moderation, facilitation, and guidance by the teacher(s)/facilitators.

Provides a Technological Environment Combining Telecommunication Systems and Computer Networks to Solve Problems of Access, Quality, and Productivity. Independence of place is achieved by being able to logon remotely to read conference postings from locations that can be determined by the user. With the appropriate hardware and network access, it is not necessary to leave job or home locations in order to attend class computer conferences. Travel-time and expense can be eliminated and inclement weather complicating travel during the winter is no longer a consideration. Both teachers and students can better organize their time around their other commitments.

Communication through CC is currently text-based (Rawson 1990; Mason 1993b), although it may change soon to include audio and video capabilities. Advantages of this text-based communication include a perception by some learners that written communication is more reflective than spoken interaction. The very act of assembling one's thoughts and articulating them in writing for a conference audience appears to involve deeper cognitive processing (Murray 1991). Additionally, students have commented that the practice in writing helps them improve their English and writing skills (Pemberton and Zenhausern 1995).

Another aspect of text-based CC is the absence of nonverbal and other social context cues associated with face-to-face communications, or to a lesser extent, telephone communications. This allows students to concentrate on the content of the message rather than the presenter (Harasim 1987). From this flows the notion of CC as an "equalizer" of persons. In a sense, the message is sans race, gender, physical appearance, shyness, physical handicap, or external social-economic and status cues (Kinner and Coombs 1995; Hiltz 1994; Selfe and Meyer 1991; Sproull and Kiesler 1991).

Access to a class conference can help the teacher manage classroom activities such as advising, evaluating, collecting and returning assignments (Hiltz 1994); and online mentoring is becoming more common (Loughlin 1993). Not only can planned events and personal networking occur, but many users of CC comment on their serendipitous experiences online (i.e., unplanned meetings or events within those that have been planned). This may occur because a user becomes involved with more kindred spirits, or forms more and varied peer and professional alliances, or might come across an opportunity for personal growth that would not have been possible without CC.

The "library" or "reference" area of a computer conference can contain several different types of files of general interest to the members, stored in read-only format. These can include readings from various sources, papers, resource lists, reference files required for the completion of classroom assignments, "help" files for assistance with using the conferencing system, bibliographies and glossaries, or even "lecture notes." Files are posted to this area by conference system staff. While they can be accessed, retrieved, read, or copied to individual storage areas, they cannot be annotated or changed by the general readership.

All messages posted within the conferencing system to private or public access work areas, which include such criteria as the author's name, the subject line, and the date posted, can be archived and then searched and/or reviewed. These archives can be used when reviewing what has been previously contributed to a specific topic. Archives can also be used to track the number and content of contributions made by conference members, thus facilitating record keeping by system staff. Archives of conference proceedings also provide a measure of security to participants in the case of personal equipment or disk storage failure.

There are other advantageous aspects of asynchronous communication for education. The combination of computer power, high-capacity storage of data, and fast telecommunication systems has led to an explosion of the use of informatics—with access to resources around the world. Instructors can plan into the syllabus the use of such resources as online public access catalogs (OPACs), commercial databases, and access to experts in the community, nation, and throughout the world. In addition, computer conferencing is a relatively inexpensive two-way communication system, provided the infrastructure of machines and networks is already accessible.

Limitations of Group Computer Conferencing

Conferencing systems have their limitations, and there are several obstacles to the use of computer conferencing today: lack of reliable access to local area networks (LANs), wide area networks (WANs), or Internet-connected hardware; technically unreliable systems; poorly designed and user unfriendly interfaces; and lack of user training and familiarity (Kaye 1989) with the hardware, software and network. Although it may be tedious for both students and teachers to become familiar with the hardware, software, and networks, teaching and learning depends on this familiarity. There is also an urgent need for expert technical support and maintenance of hardware, software, and networks. Users must practice and become familiar with their system's hardware, software, and network capabilities to the point where the technology becomes relatively transparent before they can focus on course content rather than use of the delivery system.

The amount of information accessible on the Internet is increasing exponentially and any attempt to keep up with it very quickly results in a bad case of "information overload" for even veteran users (Romiszowski and de Haas 1989). Veterans usually have developed some selection criteria to categorize incoming information, either in their own heads or explicitly as options set on their computers. However, it takes time for newcomers to develop their own classification schemes. Secondly, the more we use sophisticated systems (e.g., to deliver interactive multimedia programs requiring high technological overhead), the harder it is to avoid making class sessions place and time dependent, contrary to primary notions of distance education. That is, access to necessary systems can become problematic: it is one thing to say that technically, we can transfer digitized slides to conference members at multiple sites. It is another if each student/instructor must go to a particular computer room, during specific time periods, to view these slides because the systems that they normally use at their homes or work are not multimedia-compatible. Another limitation that has been stated is "communication anxiety" (Harasim 1990a): the contributor feels as though he or she is talking into an unresponsive vacuum. Finally, psychological as well as technological effects of computer conferencing, such as students missing face-to-face interaction, have also been explored (Kinner and Coombs 1995).

Additional limiting factors include legal issues, the need for CC moderator(s) to play a significant guiding role (Davie 1989), and the sometimes massive time investment in interaction required of both the students and teachers. The time spent developing virtual relationships may interfere with family relationships. Social use of CC, as opposed to educational use, may even be addictive (Press 1993). Finally, the text-based nature of CC favors those who are both articulate and good with the language of the discussion. All these limitations can be ameliorated with careful consideration and planning on the part of the instructional designer and systems engineers.

Changing Assumptions, Roles, and Models

While each instructional designer carries to his/her work a set of (usually implicit) assumptions about what teaching and learning should be like, I believe each of the characteristics of group computer conferencing is neutral—that is, each can be perceived as advantageous or limiting, *depending upon* the (often tacit) theories the designer/researcher holds when developing courses using CC. The activities students are asked to participate in are a function of certain models and theories about teaching and learning, and the changing roles/functions that permeate the design of courses using CC. Designers subscribing to constructivist theory might be likely, for instance, to see and use computer conferencing to design learning environments that are more authentic, situated, interactive, project-oriented, interdisciplinary, learner-centered, and which take into account the varieties of students' learning styles.

There are explicit and implicit indications in the literature of several changes in the focus of curricula and educational institutions, especially in terms of the roles of students and teachers. Instructors and designers of instruction have taken on the challenge of developing learning activities that require students to take a more active and interactive role as researcher, problem-solver, and strategist (Siegel and Sousa 1994). The trend is generally toward a more *learner-centered* approach and attitude to learning in all educational settings. Students work with other students to learn interpersonal and multi-cultural cooperation and to practice the roles of leader, collaborator, and follower. Through these collective assignments students experience becoming members of a group (Vygotsky 1978, in Fowler and Wheeler 1995). As learning environments become more technology-rich, faculty can learn to encourage and guide students in using the information resources that are available and to guide appropriate *collaborative work* (Harasim 1989, 1990b) with other students (Twigg 1994). Tomorrow's students may behave much more like today's research faculty and possess increased independence, self-direction, and self-reliance.

There are indications in the literature of progressive change in teachers' roles regarding CC. While the teacher does not know all, he or she does know how to access information. In computer conferencing, where information is not organized hierarchically with the teacher in control, the teacher also becomes a learner. The *teacher assumes the roles of a facilitator*, a resource provider, or a research librarian rather than an expert dispensing knowledge to the student (Siegel and Sousa 1994). The transition may come as quite a stressful surprise (Gunawardena 1992). Additionally, the role of teacher as a solitary developer and deliverer of content is very slowly being replaced by a *team approach* toward course development and delivery. When it comes to designing, packaging, and delivering a course using sophisticated delivery systems, there are few faculty with the skills, knowledge, time, resources, and inclination to "do it all" themselves.

Conclusions

A review of literature shows that much has been written by practitioners describing the characteristics and advantages and some limitations of computer conferencing, and justifying its use. Less has been written about instructional design issues, with the notable exceptions of Burge and Roberts (1993), Nalley (1995), and Eastmond and Ziegahn (1995). Instructional designers' assumptions about what constitutes "good education" is mirrored in the design of the instruction.

Future Research. Educators do not often randomly assign students to treatment, non-treatment, and control groups in their research because we want to include all students in what we feel are the best practices. Still, there are many interesting and potentially productive research topics within the domain of computer conferencing. For example, if we believe group interaction is desirable, what size groups and what conditions would be best in which computer conferencing settings? By articulating the evolving roles of instructors, students, and institutions as technology pervades instructional settings, we can define a more effective or efficient research agenda. By comparing variables and investigating interactions within group computer conferencing, we hope to develop more powerful learning or instructional theory.

Another interesting line of research involves the fact that computer conferencing programs can produce complete transcripts of all interactions they have mediated. These transcripts are a rich data source and tools for their analysis need to be developed that take into account both content and discourse analysis theory and practice (Rafaeli et al. 1994).

It is time to move beyond repeated justifications for the use of computer-mediated communication and computer conferencing in education. We are not trying to replicate the traditional classroom online (Hiltz 1986; Turoff 1995). It is time also to move on from case studies and general, descriptive writings about the characteristics of computer conferencing and CMC (Beaudoin 1995). While it may take the development of new or expanded methodologies, researchers need to turn their thoughts to research in computer conferencing that answers specific questions about the conditions under which each advantage operates and how best to maximize benefits and minimize the limitations of computer conferencing.

Note: I wish to thank Mauri P. Collins, The Pennsylvania State University. She and I co-author and co-research in the field of CMC and specifically computer conferencing. My appreciation, too, for her editing multiple drafts of this review.

References

Baldwin, G. D. 1995. Computer-mediated communication and American Indian education. In *Computer-mediated Communication and the Online Classroom. Vol. 1: Overview and Perspectives,* eds. Z. L. Berge and M. P. Collins, 113–136. Cresskill, NJ: Hampton Press.

Bellman, B. L. 1992. Computer communications and learning. In *Teaching in the Information Age, The Role of Education Technology*. New Directions for Teaching and Learning, No. 51, 55–63. San Francisco: Jossey-Bass.

Beaudoin, M. 1995. Integrating experience and reflection to enhance distance education practice. [Online] DEOSNEWS, 2(2). (Archived at listserv@psuvm.psu.edu, command: get deosnews 95-00002.)

Berge, Z. L., and M. P. Collins. 1993. Computer conferencing and online education. [Online] *The Arachnet Electronic Journal on Virtual Culture* 1(3). (Archived at listserv@kentvm as berge.v1n3.)

Berge, Z. L., and M. P. Collins, eds. 1995a. *Computer-Mediated Communication and the Online Classroom: Vol. 1. Overview and Perspectives*. Cresskill, NJ: Hampton Press.

Berge, Z. L., and M. P. Collins, eds. 1995b. *Computer-Mediated Communication and the Online Classroom: Vol. 2. Higher Education*. Cresskill, NJ: Hampton Press.

Berge, Z. L., and M. P. Collins, eds. 1995c. *Computer-Mediated Communication and the Online Classroom: Vol. 3. Distance Learning*. Cresskill, NJ: Hampton Press.

Burge, E., and J. Roberts. 1993. *Classrooms with a Difference: A Practical Guide to the Use of Conferencing Technologies*. Toronto, Canada: The University of Toronto Press.

Collins, A. 1991. Cognitive apprenticeship and instructional technology. In *Educational Values and Cognitive Instruction: Implications for Reform,* eds. L. Idol and B. F. Jones, 121–138. Hillsdale, NJ: Lawrence Erlbaum Associates.

Collins, A., J. S. Brown, and S. E. Newman. 1989. Cognitive apprenticeship: Teaching the crafts of reading, writing and mathematics. In *Knowing, Learning, and Instruction*, ed. L. B. Resnick, 453–494. Hillsdale, NJ: Lawrence Erlbaum Associates.

Collins, M. P., and Z. L. Berge. 1994. Student evaluation of computer conferencing in a (primarily) audio-conferencing distance education course. In *Conference Proceedings International Distance Education: A Vision for Higher Education,* 256–275. University Park, PA: The American Center for the Study of Distance Education, The Pennsylvania State University.

Cotlar, M., and J. N. Shimabukuro. 1995. Stimulating learning with electronic guest lecturing. In *Computer-Mediated Communication and the Online Classroom: Vol. 3. Distance Learning*, eds. Z. L. Berge and M. P. Collins, 105–127. Cresskill, NJ: Hampton Press.

Davie, L. 1989. Facilitation techniques for the on-line tutor. In *Mindweave: Communication, Computers and Distance Education*, eds. R. Mason and A. Kaye, 74–85. New York: Pergamon Press.

Eastmond, D. V., and L. Ziegahn. 1995. Instructional design for the online classroom. In *Computer-Mediated Communication and the Online Classroom: Vol. 3. Distance Learning*, eds. Z. L. Berge and M. P. Collins, 59–80. Cresskill, NJ: Hampton Press.

Fowler, L. S., and D. D. Wheeler. 1995. Online from the K-12 classroom. In *Computer-Mediated Communication and the Online Classroom: Vol. 1. Overview and Perspectives*, eds. Z. L. Berge and M. P. Collins, 83–100. Cresskill, NJ: Hampton Press.

Gunawardena, C. N. 1992. Changing faculty roles for audiographics and online teaching. *The American Journal of Distance Education* 6(3):58–70.

Harasim, L. M. 1987. Teaching and learning on-line: Issues in computer-mediated graduate courses. *Canadian Journal of Educational Communications* 16(2):117–35.

Harasim, L. M. 1989. On-line education: A new domain. In *Mindweave: Communication, Computers and Distance Education,* eds. R. Mason and A. Kaye, 50–62. New York: Pergamon Press.

Harasim, L. M. 1990a. *Online Education: Perspectives on a New Environment.* New York: Praeger.

Harasim, L. M. 1990b. Online education: An environment for collaboration and intellectual amplification. In *Online Education: Perspectives on a New Environment*, ed. L. M. Harasim, 39–64. New York: Praeger.

Hiltz, S. R. 1986. The "virtual classroom": Using computer-mediated communication for university teaching. *Journal of Communication* 36(2):95–104.

Hiltz, S. R. 1994. *The Virtual Classroom: Learning without Limits via Computer Networks.* Norwood, NJ: Ablex Publishing.

Kaye, A. 1989. Computer-mediated communication and distance education. In *Mindweave: Communication, Computers and Distance Education*, eds. R. Mason and A. Kaye, 3–21. New York: Pergamon Press.

Kinner, J., and N. Coombs. 1995. Computer access for students with special needs. In *Computer-Mediated Communication and the Online Classroom: Vol. 1. Overview and Perspectives*, eds. Z. L. Berge and M. P. Collins, 53–68. Cresskill, NJ: Hampton Press.

Lehman, J. D., W. D. McInerney, and G. A. White. 1993. Seventy cups of coffee, office politics and computers or how a computer-mediated distance education course was created. In *Proceedings of the Distance*

Education Conference: Teaming Up for Success. Madison, WI: University of Wisconsin, Madison.

Loughlin, T. W. 1993. Relationships: The solitary world of CMC. [Online]. *Interpersonal Computing and Technology: An Electronic Journal for the 21st Century.* 1(1) (Archived at listserv@guvm.georgetown.edu as loughlin.ipctv1n1).

Mason, R. 1990. Refining the use of computer conferencing in distance education. In *Distance Education: Development and Access,* eds. M. Croft, I. Mugridge, J. S. Daniel, and A. Hershfield, 271–272. Caracas: International Council for Distance Education (ICDE).

Mason, R. 1991. Methodologies for evaluating applications of computer conferencing. In *Collaborative Learning through Computer Conferencing,* ed. A. R. Kaye. Heidelberg: Springer-Verlag.

Mason, R. ed. 1993a. *Computer Conferencing: The Last Word.* Victoria, BC: Beach Holme Publishers.

Mason, R. 1993b. The textuality of computer networking. In *Computer Conferencing: The Last Word,* ed. R. Mason, 23–36. Victoria, BC: Beach Holme Publishers.

Mason, R., and A. Kaye eds. 1989. *Mindweave: Communication, Computers and Distance Education.* New York: Pergamon Press.

Morrison, J. L. 1993. Empowerment by technology: Using electronic dialogue to promote critical thinking. *Business Education Forum* 47(3):13–15.

Murray, D. E. 1991. The composing process for computer conversation. *Written Communication* 8:35–55.

Nalley, R. 1995. Designing computer-mediated conferencing into instruction. In *Computer-Mediated Communication and the Online Classroom: Vol. 2. Higher Education,* eds. Z. L. Berge and M. P. Collins, 11–24. Cresskill, NJ: Hampton Press.

Pemberton, A., and R. Zenhausern. 1995. CMC and the educationally disabled student. In *Computer-Mediated Communication and the Online Classroom: Vol. 1. Overview and Perspectives,* eds. Z. L. Berge and M. P. Collins, 69–82. Cresskill, NJ: Hampton Press.

Press, D. 1993. Desperately seeking connection. In *Computer Conferencing: The Last Word,* ed. R. Mason, 231–245. Victoria, BC: Beach Holme Publishers.

Rafaeli, S., F. Sudweeks, J. Konstan, and E. Mabry. 1994. ProjectH overview: A quantitative study of computer-mediated communication, Technical Report. University of Minnesota.

Rawson, J. H. 1990 Real-time computer conferencing for distance education. In *Distance Education: Development and Access*, eds. M. Croft, I. Mugridge, J. S. Daniel, and A. Hershfield, 273–275. Caracas: International Council for Distance Education (ICDE).

Romiszowski A. J., and J. A. de Haas. 1989. Computer mediated communication for instruction: Using e-mail as a seminar. *Educational Technology* 29(10):7–10.

Santoro, G. M. 1995. What is computer-mediated communication? In *Computer-Mediated Communication and the Online Classroom: Vol. 1. Overview and Perspectives*, eds. Z. L. Berge and M. P. Collins, 11–27. Cresskill, NJ: Hampton Press.

Schrum, L. 1993. Social interaction through online writing. In *Computer Conferencing: The Last Word*, ed. R. Mason, 171–196. Victoria, BC: Beach Holme Publishers.

Selfe, C., and P. R. Meyer. 1991. Testing claims for on-line conferences. *Written Communication* 8(2):163–192.

Siegel, M. A., and G. A. Sousa. 1994. Inventing the virtual textbook: Changing the nature of schooling. *Educational Technology* 34(7):49–54.

Sproull, L., and S. Kiesler. 1991. *Connections: New Ways of Working in the Networked Organization*. Cambridge, MA: The MIT Press.

Sudweeks, F., and S. Rafaeli. 1996. How do you get a hundred strangers to agree: Computer mediated communication and collaboration. In *Computer Networking and Scholarship in the 21st Century University*, eds. T. M. Harrison and T. D. Stephen, 115–136. New York: SUNY Press.

Sweet, R., T. Anderson, and M. Halenda. 1991. Adoption and use of a computer-mediated communication system by Contact North site coordinators. *Journal of Distance Education* 6(2):64–78.

Turoff, M. 1995. Designing a Virtual Classroom.™ Invited paper presented at the 1995 International Conference on Computer Assisted Instruction (ICCAI'95), National Chiao Tung University, March, Hsinchu, Taiwan. URL: http://www.njit.edu/njIT/Department/CCC/VC/Papers/Design.html

Twigg, C. A. 1994. The need for a national learning infrastructure. *Educom Review* 29(5):17–20.

Wells, R. 1992. *Computer Mediated Communication in Distance Education: An International Review of Design, Teaching and Institutional Issues.* ACSDE Research Monograph No. 6. University Park, PA: The Pennsylvania State University, The American Center for the Study of Distance Education.

Vygotsky, L. S. 1962. *Thoughts and Language.* Cambridge, MA: MIT Press.

Vygotsky, L. S. 1978. *Mind in Society: The Development of Higher Psychological Processes.* Cambridge, MA: MIT Press.

6　Designing Online Coursework Mindfully

Karen L. Murphy

Introduction

The exponential growth of the Internet has contributed to the potential for coursework offered online. A recent article listed critical information about online degree programs at fourteen institutions of higher education in the U.S. (*Online Access* 1995). The largely unchanneled growth of the Internet and computer mediated communication (CMC) for educational purposes challenges university administrators and faculty members, as well as school administrators and teachers to offer coursework online in ways that maximize student learning. Through such resources of the Internet as gopher, ftp, telnet, and the World Wide Web (Web), people are able to communicate with others, retrieve information, and access remote services quickly and easily. And with such user-friendly browsers as Netscape and Mosaic, even children can retrieve and share information easily.

A number of researchers have discussed the recent development of cultures of computer conferencing (Harasim 1989; Hiltz and Turoff 1993; Mason and Kaye 1989) and the use of the Internet for educational purposes (Anderson 1994). Bonham, Cifuentes, and Murphy (1995) assert that because of the newness of distance education cultures, and in particular the more interactive ones like CMC, participants who don't know how to behave in this new culture may do so in inappropriate or ineffective ways. Lacking adequate experience and training, teachers are likely to prepare online coursework mindlessly. A brief discussion of the hazards of mindlessness and the benefits of mindfulness (Langer 1989) in online coursework design and an overview of the characteristics of online coursework follow. The paper continues with a review of the literature and a discussion of online coursework design. It concludes with a plea to be mindful when designing online coursework.

Mindlessness and Mindfulness

With the "hurry up and jump on the (Internet) bandwagon" approach, it would not be surprising for instructional designers in distance education settings, university faculty in traditional education, and school administrators and teachers to prepare online coursework mindlessly. Social psychologist Ellen Langer's (1989) concept of mindfulness serves as a useful construct for analyzing online course design.

> When we are behaving mindlessly, that is to say, relying on categories drawn in the past, endpoints to development seem fixed. We are then like projectiles moving along a predetermined course. When we are mindful, we see all sorts of choices and generate new endpoints. Mindful involvement in each episode of development makes us freer to map our own course. (Langer 1989, 96–97)

This quotation from Langer's book *Mindfulness* illuminates the dimensions of mindlessness and mindfulness in everyday life. The hazards of mindless design and the benefits of mindful design of online courses are outlined next.

Mindlessness is characterized by the entrapment by categories, responding with automatic behaviors, and acting from a single perspective (Langer 1989). An example of mindlessness in traditional education is the way that teachers tend to teach in the same manner in which they were taught. Tally and Grimaldi (1995) posit the view that teachers, having become socialized into a set of institutional norms and values about education, maintain their views on how students and teachers should behave, and what classrooms should look and sound like. Trapped by previous categories of teaching, the typical American K-12 teacher is the "strategic, pivotal figure" (Goodlad 1984, 108) who adheres to the lecture mode. Additionally, requiring students to use rote memorization rather than apply their knowledge to other situations does little to engage students actively in their learning and reflects a single perspective about teaching.

According to Murphy (1995), the mindless approaches of lecturing and fostering rote memorization have more serious implications in distance environments than they do in traditional education. Not only does the use of technology in distance teaching tend to exaggerate poor teaching strategies, but also the technologies themselves pose barriers to teaching and learning. Hillman, Willis, and Gunawardena (1994, 32) assert that the "high technology devices" of distance education pose barriers to learning. Learners who are unable to interact successfully with the technology will be prevented from interacting successfully with the content, instructor, and other learners. In online courses, this "learner-interface interaction" (Hillman, Willis, and Gunawardena 1994) would prevent students unfamiliar with telecommunications from accessing the Internet or using computer conferencing to communicate with their instructor and fellow students.

Mindfulness, on the other hand, is distinguished by the creation of new categories, using non-automatic behaviors, and an openness to multiple perspectives (Langer 1989). Salomon and Globerson (1987) assert that mindful processing occurs when an individual exhibits these behaviors: withholds or inhibits the evocation of a first, salient response; examines and elaborates situational cues and underlying meanings relevant to the task; generates alternative strategies; gathers necessary information; examines outcomes; and draws new connections and constructs new structures and abstractions. Mindfulness in both traditional and distance education would lead to course design that engages learners actively, provides for collaborative learning, and is learner-centered.

Characteristics of Online Coursework

Online coursework is a form of computer-mediated communication and involves the use of a computer and a network connection (either via modem and telephone line or a "hard-wired" connection to a networked server), and communications and, sometimes, networking software. Once the tools are accessible, people can communicate with each other, transfer text and data files, and obtain and share information at times convenient to them. Online coursework generally occurs asynchronously, i.e., the class is not required to be present online at a specific time. Both Harasim (1989) and Mason and Kaye (1989) have described CMC as a powerful tool for collaborative learning and learner-centered instruction. The asynchronous nature of most online communication may be one of the more attractive aspects for coursework, as users are allowed time for reflection and off-line discussion or activities before posting a reply or completing an assignment.

Santoro (1995) has described CMC under three headings: computer conferencing, informatics, and computer-aided instruction. Much online coursework has been conducted via computer conferencing (cf., Berge and Collins 1995; Harasim 1989; Hiltz and Turoff 1993). Informatics, which deal with accessing and retrieving files from servers worldwide, are playing an increasingly important part in education. Examples of informatics in common use are online public access catalogs, interactive remote databases, and gopher, WAIS, and Web servers. With the advent of Web servers, documents can be stored as formatted text with pictures and sound, with built-in links to supporting or corroborating documents. Many K-12 schools have their students build a "homepage" for their schools and accumulate and index topic-specific information.

While most online coursework is asynchronous, real-time text-based discussions also take place. On mainframe computer systems, for example, Internet Relay Chat (IRC) can link thousands of users worldwide, small numbers of users can have interactive discussions (by "phone" on a VAX), and a Multi-User Dungeon, Object-Oriented (MOO), such as Diversity University and Athena University, enables users to participate in "virtual" conferences by connecting simultaneously to a single cyberspace address. Online synchronous communication can also occur through computer conferencing with certain conferencing software. For example, the Electronic Information Exchange System (EIES), which is proprietary software developed at the New Jersey Institute of Technology, allows users to communicate simultaneously with other users (Turoff 1995b).

Online coursework ranges from being totally online to being used merely as an adjunct to traditional teaching. Three models of online courses are: 1) online activities may comprise the entire course; in other words, the coursework may be delivered to students who have limited or no face-to-face contact with each other or with their instructor; 2) online activities may supplement a traditional face-to-face course; or 3) online activities may supplement a course that uses multiple methods, such as interactive videoconference, audioconference, correspondence, videotapes, and audiotapes.

Designing Online Coursework

With the potential to obtain, share, and create information using CMC, educators should be challenged to design online coursework mindfully—in a manner that fosters active learning and that avoids information overload, a legitimate concern in today's Internet explosion (Turoff 1995a). Wells' (1992, 10) extensive review of the literature of CMC suggests that online course design should not merely replicate face-to-face instruction, but should "constitute new and unique types of educational experiences," like parallel rather than linear discussions of course themes. The following section of the paper includes a review of the literature of four topics related to designing online coursework: 1) designing coursework in teams; 2) providing technical training to students; 3) using the Internet; and 4) designing for collaboration and learner-centered instruction.

Teamwork in Online Course Design. Designing high quality instructional materials and using them to teach distant students are complex matters that require a team approach, according to distance education practitioners and researchers (e.g., Eastmond and Ziegahn 1995; Laurillard 1993; Paulsen 1995b; Thach and Murphy 1994; Willis 1993). In fact, distance education experts who took part in a Delphi study identified collaboration/teamwork skills as the third top competency for distance education professionals (Thach and Murphy 1995). The other two leading competencies were interpersonal communication and planning skills. For more than two decades the U.K. Open University (UKOU) course team approach to the design and development of distance teaching materials at the post-secondary level has been emulated worldwide. These course teams, which typically consist of a coordinator, a course manager, authors, a tutor, and an instructional designer, work closely with producers to develop high quality instructional materials (Harry 1982). The course team approach fosters openness to a variety of perspectives (Parer 1993) and thereby supports a climate for healthy controversy (Riley 1984). The opportunity for creating multiple perspectives through the course team approach is certainly no less in designing online coursework than it is in distance education coursework utilizing older forms of technology.

Contrary to expert recommendations, most instructors design and teach their own online courses with little, if any, assistance. For example, Starr Roxanne Hiltz reports that she designs her own online courses with only the occasional help of a graduate assistant (Hiltz 1995b), and Chère Gibson was totally responsible for designing her online course "The Adult Independent Learner," though technical support was available for the students (Gunawardena et al. 1994). Assistance to faculty who design online coursework may be limited to technical training on specific computer applications.

While evidence of teamwork in online course design may exist, only isolated instances of teamwork have been reported. One such description is of Rensselaer Polytechnic Institute's replacement of large undergraduate lecture halls with studio classrooms in which fifty students at a time learn collaboratively as they use computers to solve problems. In one course, several faculty members integrate laboratory assignments into the class, while one faculty member works directly with the students (DeLoughry 1995b).

In a wide-scale online effort linking classes at several universities, faculty members compensated for the limited teamwork available for designing online courses at their own university campuses. All faculty members involved in either of two Globaled projects—semester-long computer conferences linking graduate classes at several universities in 1992 and 1993—were responsible for both integrating the online activities into their own coursework and conducting training for their students. The Globaled faculty agree that the advanced planning, collaborative planning, and organization were key to the successful operation of Globaled. Charlotte Gunawardena, coordinator of the Globaled project and overall moderator of the conference, was assisted by a technical coordinator in the moderator functions only (Cochenour, Rezabek, and Murphy 1995; Gunawardena et al. 1994; Hessmiller et al. 1995; Murphy et al. 1995; Rezabek et al. 1994; Yakimovicz and Murphy 1995).

While researchers and practitioners suggest the team approach for online coursework development, it appears that practice does not bear out the suggestion. Faculty cannot count on being part of a team effort and instead must concentrate on designing their own courses without benefit of the input of multiple perspectives from other members of a team. Without this input, the tendency for faculty may be to rely on pre-existing categories of teaching and learning instead of redefining the categories to include instructional strategies that enhance learning.

Providing Technical Training to Students. One way to reframe categories of teaching and learning is to design instructional activities that explicitly include four types of interaction: learner-content, learner-teacher, learner-learner (Moore 1989), and learner-interface (Hillman, Willis, and Gunawardena 1994) interaction. It has already been pointed out that the high technology devices present barriers to learning. Bonham, Cifuentes, and Murphy (1995) note that CMC is still in its cultural infancy. Older distance education technologies, such as correspondence courses utilizing video tape distribution, have two advantages: The older technologies have had more time for cultural integration, and they require fewer conventions about interaction because they are less interactive. Distance educators are still developing protocols and guidelines for use with the newer, more interactive technologies, including computer conferencing (Bonham, Cifuentes, and Murphy 1995). It is the "discursive" media (Laurillard 1993)—ones that support discussion between instructor and students and among the students themselves—that present the steepest learning curve to students.

Murphy (1995) points out that instructors who are either new to distance education or are using new delivery methods face the potential dual challenge of learning how to use technologies themselves while providing for student technical training. For example, in the same way that instructors teaching via interactive video conference need to learn how to operate the camera and audio controls, along with the protocols for use, instructors designing online coursework must design for effective use of the online technologies (Murphy 1995). However, once an instructor has mastered an Internet resource such as Veronica to search Gopher for specific information, a new resource can be introduced, such as HyperText Markup Language (HTML), used to write information onto the Web. With technologies evolving so quickly, access to the Internet becoming more simple, and costs being reduced, potentially awesome scenarios face the online instructor.

Technical problems associated with CMC typically center on getting computer accounts, gaining access to the conferences, and posting messages accurately (Gunawardena et al. 1994; Murphy et al. 1995). Technical training for students should be an integral part of the course design. Opinion differs, however, as to the nature of the technical training, specifically: 1) who should conduct the training? 2) where should it be done? 3) when should it happen? and 4) how should the training be handled?

Who should conduct the training? Training can be done by the instructor, a technician, or a graduate student. For example, to prepare my graduate students for participation in the Globaled conference, both a graduate assistant and I provided training on both CMC and the Internet. We presented issues in a generic fashion, as the students were located at three universities, and used a variety of computer systems (Gunawardena et al. 1994). Chère Gibson, on the other hand, had a half-time project assistant who assisted in training her students for Globaled, and a 24-hour help line was provided to all students for e-mail support (Rezabek et al. 1994).

Where should training be done? The location of the training can be either on-site or off-site. In each of the Globaled classes that typically met face-to-face, training occurred on-site at the respective university, usually in a computer laboratory. Even Chère Gibson's class, which was delivered online, initially received on-site technical training (Gunawardena et al. 1994). Because my students at Texas A&M University met by interactive videoconference from three sites throughout the state, technical training was presented initially via video conference, and any subsequent support occurred at the students' campuses. In addition, technical training is frequently available via the Internet. We can receive technical training from listservs (e.g., Gopher workshops by Thomas Copley) and from MOOs (e.g., a virtual conference "Research and Pedagogy in Cyberspace II: A Conferencing Workshop for Teachers on Using the Internet" was held at the Virtual Online University). In addition, Web sites provide examples of technical training: Newcomers to online courses will appreciate both O'Donnell's (1995) sage advice on the use of the Internet, e-mail, the Web, and MOOs for university teaching (DeLoughry 1995a) and Lynch's (1995) well-conceived manual for designing Web pages that is available on the Yale University Web (DeLoughry 1995a).

When should training be done? The timing of training can vary, depending on when online activities will take place. Technical training usually occurs at the beginning of the course. For example, Globaled students were required to learn about computer conferencing at the beginning of the semester so that they could participate fully in the research and online discussions (Gunawardena et al. 1994). On the other hand, those who browse the Web for advice, such as O'Donnell's (1995) and Lynch's (1995), are not restricted by either time or place.

How should training be done? Technical training can be done in a variety of ways: tutorial, self-instruction, collaboration, student performance, and demonstration. O'Donnell's (1995) Web homepage is a form of self-instruction, while Lynch's (1995) manual about designing Web pages is more akin to a tutorial. Collaboration in technical training can occur when novice users work with more experienced users, as the Globaled students were urged to do (Murphy et al. 1995).

The design of online courses needs to incorporate technical training and support of the online student. Because many instructors are still learning the capabilities of CMC as they design their online courses, they tend to behave automatically and adhere to their previous categories about teaching rather than adopting non-automatic behaviors and creating new categories. Reflecting on the four technical training issues should assist instructors in developing multiple perspectives.

Using the Internet. The literature on educational applications of the Internet and its resources is available in both print form in weekly or monthly magazines and newsletters, journals, and books, and on the Internet. For example, both Judi Harris (1995) and Don Descy (1995) write monthly columns about educational applications of the Internet in magazines targeted primarily to K-12 educators: *Learning and Leading with Technology* (formerly *The Computing Teacher*) and *TechTrends*. The book *Way of the Ferret* (Harris 1994) is but one of several books written specifically for teacher educators and for K-12 teachers about educational applications of the Internet. Technical literature abounds with information about the Internet in such publications as

Wired, *On-Line Access*, *Connect*, and *PC Computing*. Even popular literature (e.g., *Business Week*, *Time*, *Fortune*, and *Scientific American*) feature articles about the Internet.

The Internet itself contains information about its educational applications and, if one looks closely enough, on online course design—through formats such as listservs (online discussion groups), through searching tools such as Veronica for Gopher sites and Archie for ftp sites, and through browsers such as Netscape for the Web. Additionally, workshops and paper presentations on applications of the Internet in education, particularly at the K-12 level, proliferate at national conferences focusing on education or technology, such as the Association for Educational Communications and Technology (e.g., Barnard and McIsaac 1995), the Society for Information Technology and Teacher Education (e.g., McManus 1995), and Telecommunications in Education (e.g., Schrum, Andres, and Odasz 1994). Thus the potential sources of information about designing online coursework using the Internet appear to be less formal than scholarly articles found in journals and chapters in books.

Designing for Collaboration and Learner-centered Instruction. Empirical research about designing coursework by delivery through computer conferences has concentrated on ways to maximize learning by fostering interaction and collaboration among students, and by providing learner-centered instruction. Both Burge (1994) and Eastmond (1994) used interview data to describe collaborative learning and the learner-centered approach in graduate classes taught by computer conferencing. Eastmond and Ziegahn's (1995) conclusions about effective instructional design of computer conferences are based on a study of a graduate class offered by computer conference. In addition, several writers have contributed to the discussion of designing computer conferences as they grappled with the effects of computer conferencing on social relationships and patterns of intellectual exchange (Grabowski, Suciati, and Pusch 1990; Harasim 1987; Kiesler, Siegel, and McGuire 1984). Studies expanding these concepts indicate that student perceptions of the social and human qualities of computer conferences depend on instructors' and moderators' creation of social presence through interaction and collaboration (Gunawardena 1995).

The research of Gunawardena and her colleagues (Cochenour, Rezabek, and Murphy 1995; Gunawardena et al. 1994; Murphy et al. 1995; Rezabek et al. 1994) regarding Globaled recognizes the value of inter-university collaborations via computer conferencing in promoting learner-centeredness and collaboration. The Globaled computer conferences, which took place in 1992 with graduate classes at four universities and in 1993 with seven graduate classes at six universities, fostered learner-centered instruction within the individual classes. Similarly, Yakimovicz and Murphy (1995) used interview and survey data along with transcripts of computer conferences to describe the ways that a graduate class in distance education conducted collaborative research by computer conference and video conference. In this case, the combination of instructor flexibility and course requirements for electronic communication led to a learner-centered approach.

Resources about designing and moderating computer conferences in academic and classroom settings include both empirical studies and theoretical writings. Empirical research that contributes to the understanding of the design of online coursework through computer conferencing can be categorized in two ways: designing for learner-centered instruction and collaboration in computer conferences; and moderating computer conferences. Additionally, a number of authors have contributed theoretical writings that assist us in understanding how to moderate computer conferences effectively.

Empirical research on moderating computer conferences is more limited than empirical research on the design of computer conferences. While a number of authors (e.g., Berge 1995; Davie 1989; Eastmond 1992; Feenberg 1989; Kerr 1986; Mason 1991; Paulsen 1995a; Rohfeld and Hiemstra 1995) offer prescriptions for moderating computer conferences effectively, few of them claim to be based on empirical studies. An exception is the work of Tagg (1994), whose survey of a graduate course describes the transition from instructor-moderated computer conferences to online discussions that graduate students assisted in moderating. An extension of Tagg's study is an analysis of the transcripts of six computer conferences moderated by graduate students, most of whom were practicing teachers, for pre-service teachers. This study culminates with guidelines for effective moderation of computer conferences by student moderators (Murphy et al. 1996).

While reports of online coursework design abound in journals, magazines, and newspapers (e.g., *The Chronicle of Higher Education, Classroom Connect, Online Access, Learning and Leading with Technology, Electronic Learning, TechTrends, Inside the Internet*), and online discussion groups (listservs and news groups), I suggest that we learn most of our design strategies from examples found while browsing the Internet. Is this a form of conducting research? It is research, but we do not often acknowledge it as such in scholarly circles. From both browsing the Web and following online discussion groups, we can get ideas about instructional activities, locate curriculum about online coursework, and see actual lessons placed on the Internet by teachers and students.

Online coursework should be designed to take advantage of the interactive capabilities of the medium and provide for collaboration and learner-centered instruction. We are reminded that the two-way interactive technologies, "while capable of providing two-way interactivity, still depend on user skill to successfully bring about interaction in an instructional context" (Wagner 1994 9). Activities that foster interaction, collaboration, and learner-centeredness can be classified according to the following issues: 1) required vs. optional, 2) individual vs. group, 3) online vs. off-line, and 4) spontaneous vs. reflective.

- Required vs. optional activities. Online activities can be required, or they can be optional. Certainly those with experience in online coursework design maintain that requiring participation in online activities ensures participation (Gunawardena et al. 1994; Harasim 1989). Eastmond and

Ziegahn (1995) note that 30% of the grade in the course was due to participation in online activities. Murphy et al. (1996) point out that when only 5% of pre-service teachers' final grades were attributed to CMC, a few students chose not to participate in computer conferences at all. The following semester the CMC activities were assigned a value of 20% of the final grades, resulting in nearly 100% participation (L. Cifuentes, personal communication, April 3, 1995).

- Individual vs. group activities. Online activities can be organized for both individuals and groups. Searching databases, Gopher, and the Web can be construed as individual activities (Paulsen 1995b). However, an individual with a Web homepage may receive messages from others who have questions or comments. For example, on each section of his homepage, Lynch (1995) solicits comments and feedback from his readers through "forms" that readers may complete. Other individual activities, such as those based on e-mail, place the individual in the context of another. The earliest, and perhaps the most simple, classification of interpersonal exchange includes keypals, electronic appearances, and electronic mentoring, all of which are highly interactive (Harris 1994, 1995). Globaled (Gunawardena et al. 1994) is an interpersonal exchange that fits the concept of a global classroom, as do the computer conferences that my graduate students moderate for pre-service teachers at Texas A&M University (Murphy et al. 1996). In both individual and group online environments, students are led to draw new connections and construct new structures and abstractions.

- Online vs. off-line activities. Online activities may provide for both on-line and off-line work. Encouraging written exercises that respond to other "students" writing generally requires both types of activities. Students read the writing sample online, perhaps downloading it to allow time for reflection, and then upload the response (Hiltz 1995a; O'Donnell 1995). A collaborative learning strategy that Hiltz (1995a) suggests is the 'seminar' in which students become teachers and are responsible for reading the material, preparing a written summary, and leading discussion on the topic. Both online and off-line work required to complete these learner-centered activities inhibits students' initial responses and promotes examination of situational cues and underlying meanings relevant to the task.

- Spontaneous vs. reflective activities. Online activities may be either spontaneous or reflective. Brainstorming and small group discussions are spontaneous, and they can actually lead to more reflective activity. A group may brainstorm a topic and then take time to evaluate it reflectively. Having students design instructional activities for other students combines both spontaneity and reflection. For example, my graduate students designed lessons to be used as a model for pre-service teachers to design for high school students. These lessons are converted to HTML and placed on a Web homepage. The spontaneity occurs when the graduate students work collaboratively in the roles of designer and learner, critiquing each other's work, while the reflection occurs as they work off-line on their projects. In computer conferences, students may reply to an issue spontaneously, or they may prefer to take time to reflect on the issue and respond later.

In summary, designing online coursework that promotes active learning and avoids information overload requires mindful behavior on the part of instructors and course designers. Teamwork in course design, technical training for students, appropriate use of the Internet, and designing for collaboration and learner-centered instruction are integral to effective online course design.

Conclusion

As Parker Rossman (1992) predicted, we are catapulting toward a "worldwide electronic university," in which a system of higher education is potentially accessible to everyone through hybrid technologies. Valuable resources are books about online coursework (e.g., Berge and Collins 1995; Harasim 1989; Mason and Kaye 1989). Other sources for the mindful design of online courses would be books that address instructional activities in education (e.g., Davis 1993), and in distance education (e.g., Kember and Murphy 1994; Lockwood 1992), which contain ideas that can be adapted for specific online applications. These ideas encourage faculty to create new categories, to employ non-automatic behaviors, and to develop multiple perspectives—all of which lead to mindful design of online courses. With the profusion of information available on the Internet, it is easy to become overwhelmed and act mindlessly. Let us remember that "the Internet recreates the 'agora' or meeting place in which knowledge is not only shared but created and recreated" (Anderson 1994, 9).

References

Anderson, T. 1994. Using the Internet for distance education delivery and professional development. *Open Praxis* 2:8–11.

Barnard, J., and M. S. McIsaac. 1995. Schools and the Internet. Paper presented at the Annual Conference of the Association for Educational Communications and Technology, February, Anaheim, California.

Berge, Z. L. 1995. Facilitating computer conferencing: Recommendations from the field. *Educational Technology* 35(1):22–30.

Berge, Z. L., and M. P. Collins, eds. 1995. *Computer Mediated Communication and the Online Classroom*, Vol. I, II, III. Cresskill, NJ: Hampton Press.

Bonham, A., L. Cifuentes, and K. L. Murphy. 1995. Constructing cultures in distance education. In *Technology and Teacher Education Annual 1995,* eds. D. A. Willis, B. Robin and J. Willis, 614–617. Charlottesville, VA: Association for the Advancement of Computers in Education.

Burge, E. J. 1994. Learning in computer conferenced contexts: The learners' perspective. *Journal of Distance Education*, 9(1):19–43.

Cochenour, J. J., L. L. Rezabek, and K. L. Murphy. 1995. CMC: Expanding the frontiers of learner-centered instruction with "Globaled." Paper presented at the Annual Conference of the Association for Educational Communications and Technology, February, Anaheim, California.

Davie, L. 1989. Facilitation techniques for the on-line tutor. In *Mindweave: Communication, Computers and Distance Education*, eds. R. Mason and A. Kaye, 74–85. Oxford: Pergamon Press.

Davis, B. G. 1993. *Tools for Teaching*. San Francisco: Jossey-Bass.

DeLoughry, T. J. 1995a. On the Internet. *The Chronicle of Higher Education*, April 14, A26.

DeLoughry, T. J. 1995b. "Studio classrooms": Rensselaer uses computers to replace large lectures in introductory courses. *The Chronicle of Higher Education*, March 31, A19–21.

Descy, D. E. 1995. All aboard the Internet: E-mail and privacy. *Tech Trends* 40(2):10–11.

Eastmond, D. V. 1992. Effective facilitation of computer conferencing. *Continuing Higher Education Review* 56(1&2):23–34.

Eastmond, D. V. 1994. Adult distance study through computer conferencing. *Distance Education* 15(1):128–152.

Eastmond, D., and L. Ziegahn. 1995. Instructional design for the online classroom. In *Computer Mediated Communication and the Online Classroom, Vol. III: Distance Learning*, eds. Z. L. Berge and M. P. Collins, 59–80. Cresskill, NJ: Hampton Press.

Feenberg, A. 1989. The written world: On the theory and practice of computer conferencing. In *Mindweave: Communication, Computers and Distance Education*, eds. R. Mason and A. Kaye, 22–39. Oxford: Pergamon Press.

Goodlad, J. I. 1984. *A Place Called School: Prospects for the Future*. New York: McGraw-Hill.

Grabowski, B., Suciati, and W. Pusch. 1990. Social and intellectual value of computer-mediated communications in a graduate community. *Journal of the Association for Educational and Training Technology* 27(3):276–283.

Gunawardena, C. N. 1995. Social presence theory and implications for interaction and collaborative learning in computer conferences. In *Proceedings of the Fourth International Conference on Computer Assisted Instruction,* S1:10–21. Hsinchu, Taiwan, ROC: National Chiao Tung University.

Gunawardena, C. N., C. C. Gibson, J. J. Cochenour, T. Dean, C. L. Dillon, R. Hessmiller, K. L. Murphy, L. L. Rezabek, and F. Saba. 1994. Multiple perspectives on implementing inter-university computer conferencing. In *Distance Learning Research Conference Proceedings,* 101–117. College Station, TX: Texas A&M University.

Harasim, L. 1987. Current applications: Teaching and learning on-line: Issues in computer-mediated graduate courses. *Canadian Journal of Educational Communication* 16(2):117–135.

Harasim, L., ed. 1989. *On-Line Education: Perspectives on a New Medium.* New York: Praeger/Greenwood.

Harris, J. B. 1994. *Way of the Ferret: Finding Educational Resources on the Internet.* Eugene, OR: International Society for Technology in Education.

Harris, J. 1995. Mining the Internet: Organizing and facilitating telecollaborative projects. *The Computing Teacher* 22(5):66–69.

Harry, K. 1982. The Open University, United Kingdom. In *The Distance Teaching Universities,* eds. G. Rumble and K. Harry, 167–186. London: Croom Helm.

Hessmiller, R., C. N. Gunawardena, C. C. Gibson, J. J . Cochenour, T. Dean, C. L. Dillon, K. Murphy, L. L. Rezabek, and F. Saba. 1995. CMC as a vehicle for collaborative research and student-centered learning in an inter-university on-line classroom: A case study. Paper presented at the Annual Meeting of the American Educational Research Association, April, San Francisco, California.

Hillman, D. C. A., D. J. Willis, and C. N. Gunawardena. 1994. Learner-interface interaction in distance education: An extension of contemporary models and strategies for practitioners. *The American Journal of Distance Education* 8(2):30–42.

Hiltz, R. S. 1995a. Teaching in a virtual classroom. In *Proceedings of the Fourth International Conference on Computer Assisted Instruction,* S14:13–21. Hsinchu, Taiwan, ROC: National Chiao Tung University.

Hiltz, R. S. 1995b. Teaching in a virtual classroom. Paper presented at the Fourth International Conference on Computer Assisted Instruction, National Chiao Tung University, March, Hsinchu, Taiwan, ROC.

Hiltz, S. R., and M. Turoff. 1993. *The Network Nation: Human Communication via Computer* (rev. ed.). Cambridge: MIT Press.

Kember, D., and D. Murphy. 1994. *53 Interesting Activities for Open Learning Courses*. Bristol: Technical and Educational Services.

Kerr, E. B. 1986. Electronic leadership: A guide to moderating online conferences. *IEEE Transactions on Professional Communications* PC29(1):12–18.

Kiesler, S., J. Siegel, and T. W. McGuire. 1984. Social psychological aspects of computer-mediated communication. *American Psychologist* 39(10): 1123–1134.

Langer, E. J. 1989. *Mindfulness*. Reading, MA: Addison-Wesley.

Laurillard, D. 1993. *Rethinking University Teaching: A Framework for the Effective Use of Educational Technology*. London: Routledge.

Lockwood, F. 1992. *Activities in Self-Instructional Texts*. London: Kogan Page.

Lynch, P. J. 1995. Yale C/AIM WWW Style Manual. World Wide Web. [Online]. Available: http://info.med.yale.edu/caim/manual/.

McManus, T. 1995. Special considerations for designing Internet based instruction. In *Technology and Teacher Education Annual 1995,* eds. D. A. Willis, B. Robin and J. Willis, 715–718. Charlottesville, VA: Association for the Advancement of Computers in Education.

Mason, R. 1991. Moderating educational computer conferencing. [Online]. DEOSNEWS 1(19). (Archived as DEOSNEWS 91-00011 on listserv@psuvm.psu.edu.)

Mason, R., and A. Kaye. 1989. *Mindweave: Communication, Computers and Distance Education*. Oxford: Pergamon Press.

Moore, M. G. 1989. Three types of interaction. *The American Journal of Distance Education* 3(2):1–6.

Murphy, K. L. 1995. The potential for mindful teaching at a distance: A dual challenge. *International Journal of Educational Telecommunications* 1(2/3):167–183.

Murphy, K. L., L. Cifuentes, A. D. Yakimovicz, R. Segur, S. E. Mahoney, and S. Kodali. 1996. Students assume the mantle of moderating computer conferences: A case study. *The American Journal of Distance Education* 10(3):20–36.

Murphy, K. L., J. Cochenour, L. Rezabek, A. F. Dean, C. Gibson., C. Gunawardena, R. Hessmiller, and A. Yakimovicz. 1995. Computer-mediated communications in a collaborative learning environment: The Globaled '93 Project. In *17th World Conference: One World Many Voices, Vol. 2,* ed. D. Sewart, 407–410. Milton Keynes: The Open University UK.

O'Donnell, J. J. 1995. New tools for teaching. World Wide Web. [On-line]. Available: http://ccat.sas.upenn.edu/teachdemo.

Online Access. 1995. Editor's choice: Online educational courses. *Online Access* 10(1):89–95.

Parer, M. S., ed. 1993. *Developing Open Courses.* Churchill, Victoria, Australia: Monash University Gippsland Campus Centre for Distance Learning.

Paulsen, M. F. 1995a. Moderating educational computer conferences. In *Computer Mediated Communication and the Online Classroom, Vol. III: Distance Learning,* eds. Z. L. Berge and M. P. Collins, 81–89. Cresskill, NJ: Hampton Press.

Paulsen, M. F. 1995b. An overview of CMC and the online classroom in distance education. In *Computer Mediated Communication and the Online Classroom, Vol. III: Distance Learning,* eds. Z. L. Berge and M. P. Collins, 31–57. Cresskill, NJ: Hampton Press.

Rezabek, L. L., M. Boyce, J. Cochenour, T. Dean, C. Dillon, C. C. Gibson, C. N. Gunawardena, R. Hessmiller, K. L. Murphy, F. Saba, and K. Weibel. 1994. CMC as learner-centered instruction: Lessons from Globaled '93. In *Designing Learner-centered Systems: 1994 Proceedings of the Ninth Annual Conference on Distance Teaching and Learning,* 169–179. Madison, WI: University of Wisconsin-Extension.

Riley, J. 1984. *The Problems of Writing Correspondence Lessons.* DERG Papers, No. 11. Milton Keynes, UK: The Open University, Distance Education Research Group.

Rohfeld, R. W., and R. Hiemstra. 1995. Moderating discussion in the electronic classroom. In *Computer Mediated Communication and the Online Classroom, Vol. III: Distance Learning,* eds. Z. L. Berge and M. P. Collins, 91–104. Cresskill, NJ: Hampton Press.

Rossman, P. 1992. *The Emerging Worldwide Electronic University: Information Age Global Higher Education.* Westport, CT: Greenwood Press.

Salomon, G., and T. Globerson. 1987. Skill may not be enough: The role of mindfulness in learning and transfer. In *International Journal of Education Research, Acquisition and Transfer of Knowledge and Cognitive Skills,* ed. E. De Corte, 623–637. Oxford: Pergamon Press.

Santoro, G. M. 1995. What is computer-mediated communication? In *Computer Mediated Communication and the Online Classroom, Vol. I: Distance Learning,* eds. Z. L. Berge and M. P. Collins, 11–27. Cresskill, NJ: Hampton Press.

Schrum, L., Y. Andres, and F. Odasz. 1994. Announcing a new pedagogy: Designing online courses Part I. Workshop presented at the Third International Symposium on Telecommunications in Education, November, Albuquerque, New Mexico.

Tagg, A. 1994. Leadership from within: Student moderation of computer conferences. *The American Journal of Distance Education* 8(3):40–50.

Tally, B., and C. Grimaldi. 1995. Developmental training: Understanding the ways teachers learn. *Electronic Learning* 14(8):14–15.

Thach, L., and K. L. Murphy. 1994. Collaboration in distance education: From local to international perspectives. *The American Journal of Distance Education* 8(3):5–21.

Thach, E. C., and K. L. Murphy. 1995. Competencies for distance education professionals. *Educational Technology Research and Development* 43(1):57–79.

Turoff, M. 1995a. Designing a virtual classroom. In *Proceedings of the Fourth International Conference on Computer Assisted Instruction,* S14:1–12. Hsinchu, Taiwan, ROC: National Chiao Tung University.

Turoff, M. 1995b. Designing a virtual classroom. Paper presented at the Fourth International Conference on Computer Assisted Instruction, National Chiao Tung University, March, Hsinchu, Taiwan, ROC.

Wagner, E. 1994. In support of a functional definition of interaction. *The American Journal of Distance Education* 8(2):6–29.

Wells, R. 1992. *Computer-mediated Communication for Distance Education: An International Review of Design, Teaching, and Institutional Issues.* ACSDE Research Monograph No. 6. University Park, PA: The Pennsylvania State University, The American Center for the Study of Distance Education.

Willis, B. 1993. *Distance Education: A Practical Guide.* Englewood Cliffs, NJ: Educational Technology Publications.

Yakimovicz, A. D., and K. L. Murphy. 1995. Constructivism and collaboration on the Internet: Case study of a graduate class experience. *Computers and Education* 24(3):203–209.

7   Distance Learner Attitudes, Demographics, and Personalities and their Relationship to College-level Course Performance

Paul M. Biner

Introduction

Over the last four years, I, along with my colleagues Dr. Raymond Dean and Dr. Marcia Summers, have been studying a variety aspects of the tele-education courses offered by Ball State University. These classes are broadcast live (one-way video) to over one hundred remote sites across the state of Indiana, and are interactive via a two-way audio system. To date, our completed research projects have reflected two general themes. First, our work has focused on the importance of assessing students attitudes about, and reactions to, their distance education courses. To this end, we developed 1) an attitudinal assessment instrument that can be used in a direct or converted fashion to monitor student reactions to their distance education courses and 2) a method whereby others can construct their own customized attitude instrument if need be. Our second primary focus has been to formulate profiles of successful (low-risk) and unsuccessful (high-risk) telecourse students in terms of attitudinal, demographic, and personality variables.

Assessing Distance Learner Attitudes

Positive distance learner reactions cannot be construed as a guarantee that student learning has taken place. On the other hand, negative reactions can both undermine program support and detrimentally affect learning. Moreover, negative student attitudes are also likely to adversely affect student retention, motivation, commitment, and program referral rates. Thus, it is important that learner attitudes be assessed in any sound distance education evaluation program. With this premise in mind, a telecourse student attitude assessment questionnaire was developed during the summer months of 1991. This questionnaire is now known in the literature as the Telecourse Evaluation Questionnaire or TEQ (see Biner 1993).

The 33-item TEQ basically assesses student reactions to a variety of facets of taking a televised university-level course. In later confirmatory factor analytic research (see Biner, Dean, and Mellinger 1994), it was found that the items of the TEQ tapped essentially seven factors or dimensions of student satisfaction with their telecourses:

1. Satisfaction with the Instructor/Instruction
2. Satisfaction with the Technology Employed
3. Satisfaction with Program Management
4. Satisfaction with At-Site Personnel
5. Satisfaction with Promptness of Material Delivery
6. Satisfaction with Support Services
7. Satisfaction with Out-of-Class Communication with the Instructor (e.g., fax, e-mail, U.S. post)

Since its inception, the TEQ has been administered to over 1,700 students enrolled in televised courses at this university, and, to our knowledge, has been administered to distance education students at, at least, fourteen other universities throughout the country, in one form or another.

Perhaps more important than the TEQ itself is that its successful development highlights the *method* that was used to construct it. That is, the questionnaire was originally published as an addendum to a four-step methodology designed to allow distance education administrators, faculty, and program personnel (i.e., nonstatisticians and nonpsychometrists) to develop their own customized, yet psychometrically-sound, attitudinal assessment instrument (see Biner 1993). This research was prompted by 1) the realization that distance education is delivered in a diverse array of combinations of media and technology and 2) the definitive lack of rigor employed in the development of previously-published attitudinal questionnaires in the field. In brief, the steps are as follows:

Step 1: Generating Items Related to Course Satisfaction

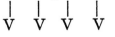

Step 2: Defining Dimensions Underlying Items

Step 3: Selecting Content Valid Items

| | | | |
v   v   v   v

Step 4: Writing and Pretesting the Instrument

Whether one uses the TEQ, in one form or another, or a self-constructed questionnaire based on this methodology, we cannot stress enough the importance of attitudinal assessment in distance education programs. Interestingly, employers have long been aware of negative ramifications of dissatisfied employees (e.g., in terms of absenteeism, turnover, apathy, productivity, and even health). Yet, in the field of distance education, the monitoring of student reactions is far from commonplace. Moreover, the programs that attempt to monitor such reactions often do so in a haphazard, ad hoc, and inconsistent fashion.

Perhaps the evaluation program here at Ball State University can be used as a model. At this institution, attitudinal data is collected from our distance education students on a semester-by-semester basis using the TEQ. Each semester, these reactions (in terms of TEQ-item means) are compared to composite reactions of the distance education students that we have had over the last several years. That is, across semesters, TEQ data has been compiled into a large database, and from this database, aggregate TEQ-item means are calculated and used as baseline measures. This, of course, allows us to efficiently pinpoint any current perceived program deficiencies, and then to intervene in some manner. For instance, two years ago, we discovered a precipitous drop in students' satisfaction with the "time the instructor left the computer-generated graphics on the screen" for copying during class. We narrowed the problem down to several of our televised MBA program courses and asked the instructors of these courses to either "slow down" or consider making copies of the graphics available to the students (which many did). Importantly, the attitudinal data gathered the very next semester indicated that the intervention had been successful.

Predicting Student Performance in Interactive Televised College-Level Courses

Our second line of empirical inquiry was prompted, in part, by the call of several investigators for more research profiling the effective or successful distance learner (e.g., Dille and Mezack 1991; Souder 1993). The general reasoning underlying this research is that, once profiles are determined, program personnel can gear their student recruitment efforts toward specific market segments. Moreover, the results of such research may also aid program personnel in identifying potentially high-risk (i.e., unsuccessful) distance education students. With this information, programs can, of course, plan appropriate and early interventions for targeted individuals, through tutoring and advising, for example, so that the chances of course failure or withdrawal are minimized.

Attitudinal, Demographic, and College/Course-Related Predictors of Course Performance. In one of our more recent studies in this area, which involved 106 undergraduate telecourse students, we attempted to assess the impact of several potential student-related predictors of student success using standard regression analyses. The predictors that were studied fell into three general categories:

- Attitudinal variables – as measured by scores on the seven factors of the TEQ
- Demographic variables – income, socioeconomic status (SES), age, and gender
- College/Course-Related variables – workload of current course, number of prior telecourses, and year in college

In line with related prior research, student success was operationalized in terms of overall course achievement (i.e., final course grades).

Attitudinal Predictors. As can be seen in Table 1, the only statistically significant attitudinal variable related to achievement was the measure of student attitudes regarding the promptness with which materials (e.g., tests, papers, and assignments) were returned by the instructor. That is, the more successful telecourse students were those who were generally satisfied with test and paper turn-around times. This result suggests that instructors should be especially attuned to returning materials to students in an expeditious fashion. The finding also converges with the findings of Rekkedal (1983), who recommended that assignment turn-around times not exceed six to seven days.

Demographic Predictors. As the correlations in Table 1 indicate, none of the demographic variables was associated with student success in the telecourses studied. That is, we found no evidence whatsoever that telecourse achievement could be predicted in any significant fashion from student gender, age, personal income, or socioeconomic status. These results are somewhat at odds with two recent and comparable investigations that empirically describe the successful telecourse student as being over twenty-five years of age (Dille and Mezack 1991) and female (Oxford et al. 1993). In light of these contradictory findings, future research is certainly warranted before any firm conclusions can be made.

College/Course-Related Predictors. Among the three potential college/course-related variables, students' year in college emerged as a significant predictor of telecourse student performance (see Table 1). That is, the most successful telecourse students in terms of achievement levels were those farther along in their college careers (i.e., juniors and seniors). From a theoretical standpoint, these students may perform at higher levels because they have a broader knowledge base than their freshman and sophomore counterparts. Of course, it

---

Table 1. Correlation of Predicator Items with Final Course Grades

Category of Item	Item	Correlation with Final Course Grade
Attitudinal Items		
	Instructor/Instruction	.11
	Technology	.17
	Program Management	.03
	At-site Personnel	.01
	Promptness of Material Delivery	.21*
	Support Services	.11
	Out-of-Class Contact	.18
Demographic Items		
	Income	-.01
	Socioeconomic Status	.17
	Age	.09
	Gender (F=1, M=2)	-.09
College/Course-Related Items		
	Workload of Course	-.02
	Number of Prior Telecourses	.14
	Year in College	.35**

* $p < .05$ (two-tailed)
** $p < .05$ (two-tailed)

is also possible that their learning strategies, which have had more time to develop, are simply better. Regardless of the precise mechanism involved, it is clear that this result suggests special caution be exercised with classes that are comprised primarily of freshmen and sophomores. For example, such telecourses could progress at a slower rate and/or special tutoring/review sessions could be offered to students to avert course failure or withdrawal.

Student Personality Variables as Predictors of Course Performance. The purpose of a second and related study, involving 164 telecourse students and 200 traditional students, was three-fold. First, we wanted to determine what personality variables, if any, were predictive of success in telecourses (with success operationalized in terms of final course grades). Our second objective was to assess the extent to which these same personality variables were related to success for a comparable group of traditionally-taught students. In the telecourses at this university, a group of traditional students attend class in the broadcast classroom on campus: they are taught by the instructor in the traditional face-to-face fashion. Finally, we hoped to compare the relative effects of personality on performance for the two groups of learners.

The Sixteen Personality Factor Questionnaire (16PF) was used to measure personality (Cattell, Eber, and Tatsuoka 1970). The 16PF is a widely-accepted personality assessment instrument with well-documented psychometric properties. The form that was employed (Form C) contains 105 items that measure sixteen bipolar personality factors. As recommended, student raw scores were converted to standardized ten-point scale (STEN) scores normed for both age and gender. Thus, these two variables were controlled for in the study.

The results, which are displayed in Table 2, show that three personality characteristics were predictive of achievement in telecourses. Moreover, two of these particular personality characteristics were found to be unrelated to course performance among students taught in a traditional manner, that is, face-to-face live instruction.

Table 2. Correlations of 16 Personality Factor Scores with Final Course Grades for Telecourse and Traditional Students

Personality Factor (Low score–High score)	Telecourse Students	Traditional Students
Cool – Warm	.04	.07
Concrete – Abstract	.06	.05
Submissive – Dominant	-.09	-.13
Tough-minded – Tender-minded	.00	.15
Trusting – Suspicious	.08	-.15
Forthright – Shrewd	.07	-.14
Self-assured – Apprehensive	.02	-.13
Relaxed – Tense	-.12	-.08
Feelings – Stable	.06	.24*
Sober – Enthusiastic	.05	-.25*
Shy – Bold	-.15	-.20*
Practical – Imaginative	.04	.28*
Conservative – Experimenting	.00	.19*
Group-oriented – Self-sufficient	.22*	.16
Undisciplined – Controlled	-.21*	.17
Expedient – Conscientious	-.48*	.28*

Note. Asterisks indicate statistical significance at $p < .01$ (two-tailed). Telecourse students $N = 164$ and traditional students $N = 200$.

One of the personality variables related to performance in telecourses was the group-oriented–self-sufficient dimension. Specifically, and quite reasonably I might add, the more self-sufficient (i.e., resourceful, independent, leadership) telecourse students tended to perform at higher levels relative to the more group-oriented (i.e., dependent, tendencies to join and follow) telecourse students. Second, the more undisciplined (or lax) students tended to earn higher grades than the more controlled (or compulsive) students. While this finding may appear counterintuitive, group comparison tests showed that the telecourse students were, in general, a highly-compulsive group of individuals (i.e., they are significantly more controlled or compulsive than the traditional students). Thus, the conclusion here may be more accurately framed by stating that extreme levels of compulsiveness tend to hinder performance in telecourses.

Finally, and perhaps the most interesting, was the finding that higher grades were associated with higher levels of conscientiousness for the traditional students, but were associated with greater expedience for the telecourse students. That expedience, as opposed to conscientiousness, works to the *benefit* of telecourse students may appear odd, at least until one considers the general life situation of these individuals. These students are typically older (Biner, Dean, and Mellinger 1994), married (Dille and Mezack 1991), and oftentimes face juggling school, work, *and* family responsibilities (Souder 1993). In light of these circumstances, it is really not surprising that high levels of expedience aid these individuals in terms of being able to functionally adapt to the diversity of work required of them. The old adage "If you want a job done well, give it to the busiest person" would certainly apply here.

Taken together, the results of this study offer potentially important information to other comparable tele-education programs, information that can be used to provide optimal learning opportunities for every student. In particular, I refer to the possibility of implementing a personality testing program in an effort to identify, from the outset of a telecourse, high-risk students, i.e., dependent, overly-compulsive, and inexpedient individuals. Once identified, such students can be persuaded through faculty advising to seek specialized tutoring, or they can be encouraged to enroll in fewer televised classes during a given semester.

Note: The research reported in this manuscript was funded by a grant from the Lilly Endowment Inc. awarded to Dr. Raymond S. Dean of Ball State University.

References

Biner, P. M. 1993. The development of an instrument to measure student attitudes toward televised courses. *The American Journal of Distance Education* 7(1):62–73.

Biner, P. M., R. S. Dean, and A. E. Mellinger. 1994. Factors underlying distance learner satisfaction with televised college-level courses. *The American Journal of Distance Education* 8(1):60–71.

Cattell, R. B., H. W. Eber, and M. M. Tatsuoka. 1970. *Handbook for the 16PF*. Champaign, IL: Institute for Personality and Ability Testing.

Dille, B., and M. Mezack. 1991. Identifying predictors of high risk among community college telecourse students. *The American Journal of Distance Education* 5(1):24–35.

Oxford, R., Y. Park-Oh, S. Ito, and M. Sumrall. 1993. Factors affecting achievement in a satellite-delivered Japanese language program. *The American Journal of Distance Education* 7(1):11–25.

Rekkedal, T. 1983. Enhancing student progress in Norway. *Teaching at a Distance* 23(Summer):19–24.

Souder, W. E. 1993. The effectiveness of traditional vs. satellite delivery in three Management of Technology Master's Degree programs. *The American Journal of Distance Education* 7(1):37–53.

Mixing It Up: Satellite Teaching and Hands-On Experience

Cheryl Achterberg

Introduction

Nutrition education is directed to Americans of all age groups. Many of the planned interventions for preschool-aged children and adults occur within the context of community programs such as the Expanded Food and Nutrition Education Program (EFNEP) conducted by the Cooperative Extension System and the Supplemental Foods Program for Women, Infants, and Children (WIC) conducted by State Departments of Health and funded by the USDA. Many of the nutrition educators in these programs are not licensed or certified; therefore, continuing education credits are not required. In fact, they may be paraprofessionals without any advanced, academic training in nutrition. Yet, the science of nutrition is moving rapidly, and professionals in the field need to stay current on the latest scientific developments. They may also need additional job skills development that prior education did not provide. Thus, continuing education is needed at the community level to improve practitioners' knowledge base as well as their delivery of services to the general public.

The challenge of delivering continuing education to community nutritionists and practitioners is heightened due to the fact that most programs have limited funds, are unwilling to release their employees for any significant length of time, and rarely send practitioners to regional or national meetings. In addition, the employees tend to be underpaid and often lack the resources to travel or enroll in additional courses themselves. Distance education, specifically short satellite conferences, appears to be a cost-efficient and potentially effective means of reaching this audience.

The purpose of this paper is to describe the theoretical base for, and results of, a satellite broadcast conference for continuing education directed to nutrition practitioners working in the field. The paper presents the theoretical premises upon which our model was based, a description of our working model, preliminary evaluation results, and a discussion.

Theory

Nutrition educators have long recognized the need for theoretical models (e.g., Brun and Rhoads 1983; Olson and Gillespie 1981; Sims and Light 1980; Achterberg, Novak, and Gillespie 1985; Smith and Lopez 1991). Most of the theories used in nutrition education, however, have been "borrowed" from the behavioral sciences with relatively few derived from education per se (Achterberg and Clark 1992). None of those in common use in nutrition education seemed especially relevant to satellite conferencing. So, our activities were informed primarily by Gowin's (1981) philosophy of education, the theory of meaningful learning (Ausubel, Novak, and Hanesian 1978) and adult learning theory (Knowles 1980). Ausubel's dictum states that the most important single factor influencing learning is what the learner already knows. The teacher needs to ascertain this knowledge and teach accordingly (Ausubel, Novak, and Hanesian 1978). Therefore, all material developed for our satellite conference was based on an extensive quantitative mail survey conducted with the potential audience as well as informal qualitative interviews with administrators in each participating agency. In addition, six well-accepted and inter-related learning principles were drawn from the literature and served as key considerations in our design and implementation decisions. These principles follow.

Learning is an active process. Meaningful learning requires effort by the learner (Ausubel, Novak, and Hanesian 1978). Although many educators contrast active and passive learning as two separate entities, their relation is relative and exists on a continuum. Purely passive or unconscious learning (e.g., biological conditioning) is relatively rare. Active or conscious learning requires the assimilation of concepts and active organization of these concepts into the existing cognitive structure. This interactive process includes adjustment of the hierarchical relationships between and among learned concepts as well as differentiation from and integration with existing relevant concepts (Ausubel, Novak, and Hanesian 1978). Rote learning, or the strict memorization of material without making meaningful connections, is merely assimilation. It is quickly forgotten. Meaningful learning that includes active integration and synthesis of new knowledge with pre-existing knowledge is remembered longer (Ausubel, Novak, and Hanesian 1978; Novak and Gowin 1984). So-called active learning, which includes audience participation and observable responses, is more efficient than passive learning, where no observable responses on the learner's part are evident (McKeachie 1963). Hence, the inclusion of discussion, other forms of interpersonal interaction, discovery learning, and experiential learning may improve learning outcomes indirectly by stimulating internal cognitive activity and meaningful learning. Lecture methods, whether in person or on television, place the learner in a passive role. However, lectures work when they are devoted to communicating meaningful materials to a highly motivated audience (McKeachie 1963).

Learning is both an emotional and intellectual process (Novak 1977; Achterberg 1988a). Mood can affect attention, the accuracy and capacity for information processing, organization of newly learned material, recall or memory, and judgment. Negative moods (vs. neutral or positive emotions and mood states) including depression, anxiety, emotional trauma, fear or other high stress states produce the greatest negative effects on performance. The effects of mood are complex, however. Sad people, for example, tend to code and recall sad events and personal experiences, especially negative experiences, better than other types of information. Negative mood states and anxiety interfere with the learning of abstract, complex, difficult, or demanding tasks. Yet, anxiety can also improve learning of simple tasks, such as eye movement (Ellis and Hunt 1993). It seems important then to create, insofar as possible, a positive, non stressful environment in which to learn, or at least to avoid the creation of any highly negative, stressful situations.

Learning requires motivation. Motivation is defined here as any stimulus, internal or external, that activates conscious or deliberate attention to, and processing of, certain incoming information. A motivated learner is aroused, focused, curious, and selective, i.e., she filters out extraneous information in order to concentrate on the information of interest. In fact, motivation and interest are tightly linked in the literature. To learn critical thinking or to process information at any higher level, students must learn to want to think (McKeachie 1963). To develop a student's interest in learning and thinking, educators need to make the experience satisfying (Wlodkowski 1985). McKeachie (1963) points out that a student's interests (i.e., motivation) are not fixed; teachers can capitalize on the motives students already have, but they can also create new motives by encouragement, posing problems within the range of their students' abilities, setting reasonable goals, and helping students to achieve. Gagne (1985) stated that motivation gives direction and intensity to behavior. Factors that modulate motivation include conflicting thoughts or uncertainty; causal attributions; emotions; expectations; and memories or prior knowledge (Gagne 1985).

Motivation is important because there is no possibility of unattended information influencing later behavior (Ellis and Hunt 1993). Hence, educators should try to motivate learners by first capturing their attention with arousing and somewhat novel stimuli. Furthermore, they should create activities that are reinforcing, fun, and interesting in order to maintain learner motivation. Ideally, learners will shift their reliance on the teacher or external stimuli for motivational purposes to self-motivation as they gain success with the new knowledge and skills presented (Gowin 1981). Information that is perceived as relevant, useful, and problem-solving is likely to be more motivational than information that is perceived as abstract, irrelevant and disconnected to the everyday problems or experiences in an adult learner's life (Ausubel, Novak, and Hanesian 1978; Knowles 1980; Wlodkowski 1985).

Concrete information is better remembered than abstract information (Paivio 1971; Clark et al. in press; von Eye, Dixon, and Krampen 1989). Paivio (1971) suggested that information is encoded in (at least) two forms, verbal codes and images. Any information that can be visualized is coded in images whereas abstract information that can be described, but not pictured, is coded verbally. Information that is coded in images is called concrete. It is easier to recall than verbal information, but information that is coded in both systems is recalled even better. Hence, to maximize learning, information should be presented in a concrete form whenever possible but, ideally, it should be presented both verbally and in images to assist learners in coding it.

People acquire behavior patterns by observing others (Bandura 1977), *practicing the behaviors* (McKeachie 1963; Prochaska, Norcross, and DiClemente 1994), *and receiving feedback on their performance* (Gagne 1985; McKeachie 1963). Students have a tendency to learn from teachers' behaviors and to model those behaviors especially when the teacher is well liked and respected (Gagne 1985). Other students can also provide effective models of desirable behavior. However, if students are to learn skills, they have to practice the skills (McKeachie 1963). Actual sensorimotor experience is more effective in learning perceptual or motor responses than verbal description. Yet, practice works only if the learner sees the results of his or her practice (McKeachie 1963). Feedback is essential. Feedback helps the learner to stay on task, change course as needed, reinforce the learner's effort(s), and motivates improvement (Eble 1965).

Theory and practice should be connected in the educational experience, not left to chance. (Bronfenbrenner 1979; Achterberg 1988b). Research evidence suggests that what a learner learns in one context is not necessarily applied in another context unless the learner is specifically motivated to do so. The likelihood of such application will also increase if the learner can anticipate and diminish barriers in the new environment (see motivation, above). Bandura (1977) suggests role rehearsal for each environment. Whatever method is employed, it is important then to teach skills in a manner that connects as directly as possible to the environment where those skills should be used.

A Working Model: Teaching and Delivery Methods

The traditional approach for continuing education with community nutritionists and practitioners is the lecture presentation or small group approach. This strategy allows for ample opportunity for interactivity and rapport building between the instructor and the learner participants as well as effective monitoring of their progress. Adjustments in the presentation can be made on an "as needed" basis. In addition, the format is familiar to instructors and learners, and it might increase a learner's sense of security or comfort with the environment and, therefore, indirectly with the material. The traditional format has certain obvious disadvantages, however. For example, only a limited number of students can be reached at once and there is a high cost in personnel and time. The method can also be faulted for poor standardization if it is delivered by different people at different points in time, or even if it is delivered by the same person at different points in time. As pointed out earlier, this format is also considered inconvenient for both practitioners and their employers, as well as the instructors. Finally, depending on the location, traditional classes may be inaccessible, especially to practitioners residing in rural areas.

Satellite broadcast seemed like an attractive alternative vehicle to deliver nutrition education to community practitioners because of its potential to reach a large number of learners and provide continuing education in a relatively convenient, accessible and cost-effective manner (i.e., down link sites could be located near the place of employment, a minimum amount of time away from the clinic would be required, and travel and other training costs would be minimized). At the same time, more learners could be provided with direct access to professional expertise, the providers' time and resources could be used more effectively (on a per student basis), and the format might appeal to autonomous adult learners. However, it was recognized that satellite broadcast is also characterized by certain disadvantages; students are passive, the medium does not facilitate problem solving, the format may be unfamiliar and/or unappealing to many adult learners (especially if it does not match the quality of commercial television broadcasts), it is difficult to check learners' progress, and it may increase feelings of insecurity among adult learners who are unpracticed with the format. In addition, satellite broadcast is very demanding of, and often uncomfortable for, the instructors.

Thus, a mixed model was created that combined satellite sessions with small group, hands-on, activity sessions. This model was created to correct or adjust for many of the disadvantages associated with satellite and traditional delivery systems while maximizing the advantages associated with each. The mixed model was designed to present basic, didactic-type information by satellite in brief segments lasting from forty-five minutes to an hour and a half. Then, learners applied that information in problem solving or experiential learning situations at their site for forty-five minutes to an hour and a half. Local site activities were overseen by facilitators trained by the conference organizers. After the learning experiences, question and answer sessions with "the experts" were provided in "real time" by broadcast, and the next informational segment was delivered via satellite. The conference proceeded in this back and forth or up and down manner throughout two days.

This mixed model addressed the learning principles outlined above more effectively than either model alone could, and it provided the needed learner support for this audience. Specifically, the mixed model allowed learners to develop personal rapport with, and receive feedback from, their local facilitator. It also allowed the organizers to reach and dialogue with more learners in a more cost effective manner. Both formats provided motivation. The mix of formats allowed the organizers to present and model desired behaviors, and the learners were able to practice the desired behaviors on-site after observation. The learning tasks were constructed for active learner involvement, the presentations were made as concrete as possible with both visual and supportive text information available, and the material was organized in a sequential, spiraling manner based on an extensive survey of the audience's perceived needs and knowledge base. During the course of content presentation, attention was given to producing as professional a broadcast as possible, including background scenery, props, chyron, a moderator, panel discussions, roll-in films, and illustrations.

Evaluation Results

Three continuing education conferences for community nutritionists have been conducted by the Penn State Nutrition Center. The first conference was conducted in the traditional face-to-face manner at Penn State in 1991 with about 100 participants. The second conference used the mixed model approach in 1992 and was broadcast to six sites across Pennsylvania and in Washington, D.C. It also reached about 100 participants. The third conference was broadcast to twenty-one sites across the Commonwealth of Pennsylvania in May 1994. Over 500 participants attended this conference. A fourth conference using this mixed model was broadcast in May 1995. It was broadcast to five states and 580 attended. This paper will focus on the results from our experience in May 1994.

The May 1994 conference was entitled Bridge II–Building Communication Bridges. There were a total of 571 participants. Attendance ranged from 10 to 75 participants/site with a mean of 27.7 participants/site. The effectiveness of the teleconference was evaluated using two questionnaires: a pre-conference questionnaire administered at the beginning of the conference and a post-conference questionnaire administered immediately after the conference. All questionnaires were developed according to Dillman's (1994) survey methodology. The evaluation questionnaires were designed to ask a number of identical questions to facilitate comparison. Some of the survey questions were open-ended, but most were close-ended with ordered response choices. The questionnaires were developed to survey participants' knowledge, attitudes, and opinions about the conference and its topic, and to gather additional demographic information. There were 546 usable evaluation forms returned. Only one site did not return evaluation forms.

Participants were employees of EFNEP and Cooperative Extension (15%) or WIC (85%). The vast majority (94.7%) were women and most were Caucasian (60.6%). About one-fourth (23.6%) were African-American. About one-fourth had a high school diploma (25.6%), another quarter (27.3%) had 1–2 additional years of schooling beyond the high school diploma, and another fourth (25.9%) had 15–16 years of schooling. Most participants (62.3%) were satisfied with their jobs. Almost 60% of the participants rated communication skills as "very important" to their work and most (67.6%) rated their level of knowledge about the topic as "average." Thus, the conference topic was relevant to the audience and their needs.

In terms of convenience, only 24% of the participants rated the conference "inconvenient" or "very inconvenient" whereas 54% of the group rated the meeting "convenient" or "very convenient." Most were required by their supervisors to attend (i.e., they had no choice). Over 80% of the group traveled less than 60 minutes to attend the meeting. On a scale of 1–5 (1=low; 5=high), participants rated the importance of an instructor being physically present as 3.1 (i.e., neutral) before the conference and 3.3 afterwards. Only 11.2% were "uncomfortable" or "very uncomfortable" with a conference delivered by satellite broadcast at the outset; this was reduced to 9.2% afterwards. The participants expected to learn a "medium" amount (mean response = 3.6 on a 5 point scale) before the conference began and reported learning a "medium" amount (mean response of 3.7 on a 5-point scale) when it was completed. However, 46.2% reported they knew a "great deal" about the topic after the conference vs. only 16.2% before the conference began. The overall quality of the conference, including sound, video quality, quality of printed material, local host's effectiveness, and registration procedures, was rated 4.0 on a 5-point scale.

Discussion and Conclusion

Based on our prior experience and data about the conference described, we conclude that this audience learned at least as well via our mixed satellite and hands-on learning conference as the audience in a conference that combined face-to-face didactic lectures and small group activities. We believe the success for this satellite approach is due, at least in part, to the mixed model being grounded in the learning principles presented in this paper. Audience expectations greatly affected the perception of conference outcomes as suggested by the motivational research literature (Gagne 1985). The audience was not discouraged or disappointed by the satellite broadcast or mixed model presentation, nor were they intimidated by it beforehand. In sum, it can be argued that the learners received as much from and felt as good about the mixed model presentation as they did from a traditional face-to-face presentation three years earlier. Thus, a mixed-model satellite approach appears to be justified for continuing education for nutrition community practitioners in the future based on cost effectiveness, reach, convenience, and time factors. It is also recommended that this same model be tried with other continuing education programs in a variety of disciplines.

However, the question remains on how to improve learning outcomes beyond traditional expectations using this newer format and approach. Moore (1991) noted that distance education creates a physical separation that leads to a psychological and communications gap between the instructors and the learners. We tried to address this gap by including many opportunities for dialogue with the presenters as well as more personalized instruction and feedback from on-site facilitators. Almost certainly, the personalities and preparation of the on-site facilitators varied among sites and affected their impact. However, little time was spent on training the facilitators about the educational philosophy underpinning our mixed model approach. Thus, the facilitators' perspectives may have greatly affected the delivery of support on-site. Training of facilitators will be expanded and modified for our 1995 conference, primarily to improve local communication and support. Written and oral presentations will address the philosophical underpinnings for the general audience of learners as well.

Considerable attention was given to Moore's (1991) variables of structure and dialogue. Structure was provided to enable learners to discern the intent of the conference and to provide a framework for marking their own progress and involvement. This was considered especially important for the para-professionals involved in the conference who may be unfamiliar or otherwise uncomfortable with more autonomous forms of learning. At the same time, considerable flexibility was built into the question and answer (Q&A) and local sessions to address learners' issues as they arose. Learners were able to dialogue with each other at their local sites, with learners at other sites, and with the conference providers. Thus, it seems unlikely that adjustments in structure or dialogue will result in major differences in learning outcomes. Furthermore, it is very uncertain whether providing more learner autonomy would make a difference given the relatively low motivational characteristics of the audience.

It appears more likely to this author that learning can be improved to the degree that the content itself is improved, i.e., made more meaningful to the audience (Ausubel, Novak, and Hanesian 1978; Knowles 1980; Wlodkowski 1985). Presentation plays a role, but presentation may not be the central issue. Rather, the meaning and usefulness of the potential application may be of paramount importance. This brings us to Gowin's (1981) four educational commonplaces: teacher, learner, curriculum, and governance, where governance includes both the physical environment and the rules that determine actions and relationships within the environment (Achterberg 1988b). Presentation is a part of governance in that it plays a role in making the connections between learners, instructors, and the curriculum. Regardless of the presentation format, the learners' characteristics, the teacher's characteristics, or the teacher's knowledge of the learners, instruction will suffer if the curriculum is less than it can or should be. Hence, at least as much attention should be given to the content in distance education as is given to the delivery mechanism and other structural components. More important, however, is the need to examine the interactivity of all the variables in the four commonplaces. This will require a systems approach. To paraphrase Bronfenbrenner (1979), the interaction among the four commonplaces is more important than any action within a commonplace.

In conclusion, distance education can indeed be informed by general educational theory and philosophy. The need for a separate theory is not self evident. If anything, distance education stretches some of the variables in the traditional models we have used in the past, but this investigator fails to see how the variables, process, or outcomes are fundamentally different in distance education from other educational enterprises. As Shale (1990, 334) states:

---

distance education ought to be regarded as education at a distance. All of what constitutes the process of education when teacher and student are able to meet face-to-face also constitutes the process of education when teacher and student are physically separated.

Present technologies that offer two-way, real-time communication, such as teleconferencing, bridge the gap of physical distance between teacher and students. The differences that exist between teaching at a distance and teaching face-to-face still need particular attention, but do not warrant the development of a theory. However, the need for careful theory-driven research, based on already existing theories, is more important than ever. Evaluations should be planned and conducted accordingly.

References

Achterberg, C. 1988a. Factors that influence learner readiness. *Journal of the American Dietetic Association* 88:1426–1428.

Achterberg, C. 1988b. A perspective on nutrition education research and practice. *Journal of Nutrition Education* 20(5):240–243.

Achterberg, C., and K. L. Clark. 1992. A retrospective examination of theory use in nutrition education. *Journal of Nutrition Education* 24:227–233.

Achterberg, C., J. D. Novak, and A. H. Gillespie. 1985. Theory-driven research as a means to improve nutrition education. *Journal of Nutrition Education* 17:179–183.

Ausubel, D. P., J. D. Novak, and H. Hanesian. 1978. *Education Psychology: A Cognitive View*. 2nd ed. New York: Holt, Reinhart, and Winston.

Bandura, A. 1977. *Social Learning Theory*. Englewood Cliffs, NJ: Prentice-Hall.

Bronfenbrenner, U. 1979. *The Ecology of Human Development*. Cambridge, MA: Harvard University Press.

Brun, J. K., and A. F. Rhoads, eds. 1983. *Nutrition Education Research: Strategies for Theory Building* - Conference Proceedings. Rosemont, IL: National Dairy Council.

Clark, K. L., C. Achterberg, A. von Eye, and R. AbuSabha. In press. Text and graphics: Manipulating nutrition brochures to maximize learning. *Health Education Research: Theory and Practice*.

Eble, R. L. 1965. *Measuring Educational Achievement*. Englewood Cliffs, NJ: Prentice-Hall.

Ellis, H. C., and R. R. Hunt. 1993. *Fundamentals of Cognitive Psychology*, 5th ed. Dubuque, IA: Brown and Benchmark.

Gagne, E. D. 1985. *The Cognitive Psychology of School Learning*. Boston: Little, Brown, and Co.

Gowin, D. B. 1981. *Educating*. Ithaca, NY: Cornell University Press.

Johnson, D. W., and R. T. Johnson. 1985. Nutrition education: A model for effectiveness, a synthesis of research. *Journal of Nutrition Education* 17:S1–S44.

Knowles, M. S. 1980. *The Modern Practice of Adult Education: From Pedagogy to Andragogy*. Chicago: Follett.

McKeachie, W. J. 1963. Research on teaching at the college and university level. In *Handbook on Research on Teaching*, ed. N. L. Gage, 1118–1172. Chicago: Rand McNally.

Moore, M. G.1993. Editorial: Distance education theory. *The American Journal of Distance Education* 5(3):1–6.

Novak, J. D. 1977. *A Theory of Education*. Ithaca, NY: Cornell University Press.

Novak, J. D., and D. B. Gowin. 1984. *Learning How to Learn*. Cambridge, NY: Cambridge University Press.

Olson, C., and A. H. Gillespie, eds. 1981. Proceedings of the workshop on nutrition education research. *Journal of Nutrition Education* 13: S1–S118.

Paivio, A. 1971. *Imagery and Verbal Processes*. New York: Holt.

Prochaska, J. O., J. C. Norcross, and C. C. DiClemente. 1994. *Changing for Good, The Revolutionary Program that Explains the Six Stages of Change and Teaches You How to Free Yourself from Bad Habits*. New York: West Morrow.

Shale, D. 1990. Toward a reconceptualization of distance education. In *Contemporary Issues in American Distance Education,* ed. M. G. Moore, 333–343. Oxford: Pergamon Press.

Sims, L., and L. Light, eds. 1980. *Direction for Nutrition Education Research-The Pennsylvania State University Conference Proceedings*. University Park, PA: Pennsylvania State University.

Smith J. L., and L. M. Lopez. 1991. The application of theory and its relationship to program effectiveness in nutrition education research. *Journal of Nutrition Education* 23:61–64.

von Eye, A., R. A. Dixon, and G. Krampen. 1989. Text recall in adulthood: The roles of text imagery and orienting tasks. *Psychological Research* 51:136–146.

Wlodkowski, R. J. 1985. *Enhancing Adult Motivation to Learn*. San Francisco, CA: Jossey Bass.

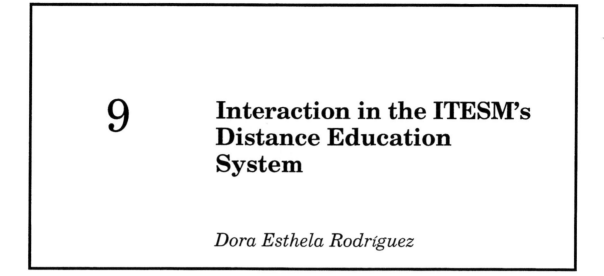

9 Interaction in the ITESM's Distance Education System

Dora Esthela Rodríguez

Introduction

The Monterrey Institute of Technology (ITESM), Mexico, founded in 1943, is today a multi-campus university system unique in Latin America in both size and complexity. This system is composed of twenty-six campuses in twenty-five cities with a faculty of 1,658 full-time professors and 2,791 part-time professors and a student body of 63,000. It offers thirty-two undergraduate programs, thirty-eight graduate programs, and six doctoral programs.

In 1989, in order to meet ITESM's goals in faculty development and to take advantage of the opportunity to use new technologies in communications, the Satellite Interactive Education System (SEIS) began broadcasting undergraduate and master's programs courses, as well as continuous education programs. The courses were broadcast via two independent transmitting channels at the Monterrey and Mexico City campuses.

ITESM's Satellite Interactive Education System or SEIS (Sistema de Educación Interactiva por Satélite)

Technological Elements of SEIS. SEIS is a distance education system based primarily on the transmission of live classes via satellite link. Courses are offered live because interaction is possible during class time through an on-line computer network. Thus the 'interactive' label of the system.

Classes are not delivered from traditional television studios, but rather from special classrooms that attempt to be as similar as possible to the traditional classroom. The classroom is equipped with four small remote-controlled cameras located on the four upper corners of the room, and their operation goes practically unnoticed by both students and teacher. There are several small wide-range microphones throughout the classroom that allow the professor and students to speak freely, without having to speak directly into a particular microphone.

Nevertheless, there are several characteristics of the transmitting classroom that clearly set it apart from traditional classes. Since there is no blackboard, the professor has little chance to develop his/her notes, diagrams, outlines, etc. in class as the explanation is going on. Therefore, he/she must prepare all graphic materials beforehand, so they can be presented to the students in one of the following ways: 1) a chromakey projection board (such as the one used by weather forecasters), 2) electronic material broadcast directly from a computer, or 3) printed material placed on the professor's desk and transmitted via an overhead camera. This last resource also gives the professor the opportunity to elaborate handwritten material during the discussions, but the use of such unplanned, visually poor material is not encouraged. On-site students in the transmitting classroom are able to see the materials on several monitors distributed throughout the room. In this sense, they are in circumstances equal to those of their remote classmates.

Means of Interaction. In addition to a monitor where the professor can see him/herself and the materials being televised, the classroom also has a computer terminal. Through the online computer network, known as IRS (Interactive Remote System), the professor has access to the incoming questions or comments from the remote students. The questions and comments do not arrive directly to the professor's terminal. They are filtered by a moderator outside the classroom who decides what is pertinent to the discussion that is going on. This moderator (who is generally the professor's assistant for that course) is necessary for the following reasons: First, it would be impossible for the professor to answer incoming messages from all students willing to participate, considering that some classes have about 150 students enrolled at the graduate level and 1400 at the undergraduate level. Second, a considerable percentage of the incoming messages are not content-oriented, such as questions about due dates, grading, office hours, etc. These would in no sense be relevant to class discussion. They are answered directly by the moderator. Finally, our first experiences showed us that even content-oriented messages could have negative effects if left unfiltered. There might be incoming messages related to topics that had already concluded in the ongoing lecture/discussion. Responding would force the professor to open the discussion again, sometimes at the expense of more important topics still left to be discussed. The moderator could decide if such questions/comments were worth considering during the remaining class time, and if not, could print them and hand them to the teacher after class, so that he/she could contact the students during office hours.

Electronic mail communication is yet another important means of interaction between the professor and distant students in addition to the online data network and the more traditional telephone/fax connection. Every distance course in SEIS is allotted an off-line e-mail address and a moderated discussion group. The first allows for individualized contact between teacher and students as often as necessary. Every student receives an e-mail address and can contact the professor or classmates in other towns. This is the most reliable counseling means; it is not expensive, it is available twenty-four hours a day (since it is not online), and it is not limited in the length of the messages that can be transmitted.

This network offers the possibility of carrying out a class discussion outside the classroom as well as individual counseling. The professor can, for instance, ask the students in Saltillo and Guadalajara to post their opinions on a certain topic discussed in class or in the required readings. The teacher receives these opinions in his/her e-mail mailbox and decides which are worth posting in a discussion group created exclusively for the course. This is a read-only posting available to all enrolled students. The professor can then ask the students in Chiapas and Zacatecas to reply to the opinions of their classmates and thus get a discussion under way, establishing an indirect interaction among the students.

As mentioned earlier, our televised courses began in the Fall term of 1989 with the idea that we should try to transfer all the elements of the traditional classroom to the television studio. Our review of the literature on distance education and our visits to several American universities with distance education programs had shown us that one of the most differentiating aspects between face-to-face and distance courses was the lack of on-time significant interaction between the students and the professor in the distance courses. Since we had the required technology to facilitate interaction among remote students during the live sessions, we thought the class could truly become a no-walls classroom, with remote students interacting just like the on-site ones. We even incorporated our traditional class format of two weekly 90-minute sessions or three 50-minute sessions.

To our surprise, remote interaction turned out to be much more difficult to handle than expected, and the classroom dynamics were completely different than those in a traditional class, even if the technology allowed for on-line "instant" interaction. First, the on-site students seemed to be inhibited by the studio hardware and the awareness that whatever they said would be seen and heard live in twenty-six other "classrooms." Remote students, on the contrary, seemed to be perfectly comfortable with the anonymous status that interacting via computer networks offered them, and their participation was unpredictable. For example, they would promptly answer or post certain questions on topics being treated by the teacher; they would suddenly ask questions about a topic that had been explained twenty or thirty minutes before, forcing the professor to go back in his/her lecture; or they would be utterly silent, unwilling to answer certain questions necessary for the correct functioning of the class delivery. Additionally, a considerable percentage of the questions that were sent to the professor were not related to the class content but to more administrative aspects of the course.

The Master's in Education Program

The main goal of the Master's in Education program is to provide professors working at the university level the necessary knowledge and skills to improve their teaching practice in a specific content area. The program consists of a research training seminar and twelve courses: six in the education area, and six in one of the following ten content areas of Applied Linguistics, Architecture, Biology, Chemistry, Communications, Cognitive Development, History, Law, Mathematics, or Physics.

The program has been offered since the Summer of 1989. During the first four years, the education courses (the core courses common to all students) were delivered via satellite, while the specialty area courses were offered as on-site intensive summer seminars. Since the Fall term of 1992, all course have been offered via satellite, except for those in the Law and Physics areas, where the number of students has remained very low. Also, Architecture, Biology, and Chemistry were specialty areas offered only during four summers, since they were originally created to meet the needs of small undergraduate programs in the ITESM System, which were practically covered by 1992.

As in all other SEIS programs, the interaction between faculty and students in our master's program has relied on off-line and online electronic mail, as well as the telephone and fax. Through these technologies students and professors have the opportunity to interact during class sessions and to carry on the interactions outside of class.

Student Perceptions of Interaction[1]

To briefly analyze how students view interaction, I will present data from our very first students. These data were obtained from a survey which contained fifteen open and closed questions. The characteristics of the sample group of thirty-six students and their distribution follows. Seventeen students were enrolled in the Summer session of 1989, eight were enrolled in the Fall semester of 1989, and eleven in the Summer session of 1990. Ninety percent of the students were between the ages of twenty-six and thirty. Half of the students were women and half were men. Sixty percent of the students' work load was dedicated to teaching. The percentage of students enrolled in the various content areas follows: 44% were enrolled in the History and Mathematics specialty area, with 22% in each area; 17% were enrolled in Applied Linguistics; and 13% of the students were enrolled in Communications and 13% in Cognitive Development. At that time, Architecture and Biology were not being offered.

Responses from the survey indicated that for 72% of the sample group, effective interaction implies that professors know what their students think of them because 1) effective interaction is only possible among equals (34%) and 2) professors can use student feedback to design a better teaching-learning process (34%).

When asked what advantages resulted from effective interaction between professors and students, the students responded as follows:

- 67% - Enhances communication
- 50% - Allows for professors and students to identify their assets and their errors
- 47% - Improves professors' teaching
- 42% - Informs professors, through student questions, about students' interests and ways of thinking
- 33% - Increases student interest in content matter

Eighty-one percent of the students thought effective interaction was possible despite the distance and the necessary technology. Although 14% did not indicate how this interaction could be achieved, 61% said that effective interaction was possible if the electronic mail was used with this goal in mind. Eight percent thought that interaction was more effective during the class session and in the feedback professors gave them in their written essays. Fourteen percent thought interaction was not possible due to 1) the time span between their questions and the professor's answers, and 2) the lack of personal, face-to-face interaction.

These opinions suggest the need of distant students for personal interaction in their first experience with distance education. Did the professors foster interaction? Sixteen percent of the students indicated they did, while 73% reported the media was used fairly regularly by professors for interaction, and 11% scarcely used it. Of the 84% who used the media only regularly or scarcely, 44% said that their communication with the professor was not constant nor permanent. One half of the students said that it was due to the distance between them. The other half reported that it was difficult to get answers to their questions, either because the professor was not available or because they had to wait for the professor to respond during a pause in the class session. They found this very frustrating in comparison to a traditional class were students can usually interrupt the teacher and receive an immediate answer.

Since most of the interaction was related to clarifying doubts about student assignments, and our intent was to facilitate more content-oriented discussion, we decided to design written self-study materials for each distance course. By 1992, all courses offered via satellite had a self-study guide or manual: Six education courses, and four courses in each one of the content areas of Applied Linguistics, Communication, Cognitive Development. At present, seventeen courses in those areas have their own "Manuals."

The new materials which were developed not only decreased the number of questions related to the assignments, but they enabled us to decrease our use of satellite time, reducing our courses to one three-hour session every two weeks. Last but not least, higher academic levels of student-professor and student-student interaction were achieved.

In the future the Master's in Education faculty will be developing multimedia software for each of the education area courses, as a part of a Virtual University Program that has been planned at the ITESM System level.

Types of Interaction[2]

In this section, I will analyze the following types of interaction:

- Student and delivery media interaction
- Student and instructional materials interaction
- Student and electronic mail interaction, compared with traditional face-to-face interaction

These aspects will be presented in terms of the following variables: 1) access to the technology and 2) readiness for the adequate use of the technology.

Interaction between Students and the Delivery Media. For the interaction between students and delivery media, I refer to information from the Fall semester of 1989 when our program began. At the time, we offered the students living in Monterrey, the uplink site of our delivery system, the option of taking the course in the delivery classroom or in a traditional classroom. Eighty percent chose the traditional classroom. Let me elaborate on this. The faculty made this request because they had no idea of what problems they would face in the satellite courses. They felt a little safer having a familiar, traditional classroom, too. Obviously, the existence of the two options was beneficial for those students who were anxious about the technology in the studio-classroom. They could choose to attend the traditional class. In comparing the achievement of the students in the distant classroom, on-site traditional classroom, and on-site studio classroom at the end of the term, the faculty were convinced that distant students learned more, in a more significant way, and with less effort than their on-site peers.

A second problem which caused concern at the beginning of the term was use of the technology. The faculty were more or less adequately prepared to use the delivery technology, but were the students?

During that first semester, for instance, only students interested in technology or innovative students, eager to try new methodologies, chose to be in the delivery classroom. However, by the fourth class session even those students who chose to be in the class had serious problems participating. When asked why they spoke so little, most of them replied they were inhibited by the fact that anything they said was being seen and heard at the national level. The idea of saying something wrong or silly was too overpowering. Nevertheless, by their third course in the delivery classroom environment most of them felt free to participate. On the contrary, remote students felt much more at ease in their classrooms and participated frequently through questions and comments during the class session. We still do not prepare our new students to handle inhibition in the delivery classroom, but since satellite courses have become a part of student culture at the ITESM, we find that every term fewer students seem to have problems with "speaking at the national level."

Our distance students, on other hand, do have an orientation session, since they must learn to handle much more technology than their on-site peers in order to interact effectively. This session is organized by our local administrative coordinator (one at each of the twenty-six campuses). It includes a video with an brief explanation of how our program works, and a description of the most frequent "problems" of being a distant student, as well as some suggestions on how to overcome them.

The ITESM System offers training courses for faculty who deliver classes via satellite. A TV producer and a designer are also assigned to each professor one semester before the course is scheduled for delivery, since all didactic materials are computer designed. Thus the entire course can be planned and designed before the first class is broadcast.

Interaction between Students and the Instructional Material. As I pointed out earlier, originally we had not included printed instructional materials, other than a bibliography, in our design for courses to be delivered via satellite through SEIS. Nevertheless, the lack of these materials created several problems. Most of the online interaction during class revolved around due dates and instructions for papers, which reduced student participation and interaction on the content of the course. Also, students requested that the written materials used by the professor during the class be left on screen longer so they could copy the information. This used costly broadcasting time, when the material could have been sent beforehand, so the students could have them in time for class discussions. We realized the need to provide three types of written materials for the students: 1) the materials used by the professor in his/her presentations to the class, 2) a guide including not only the professors' interpretation of the content but also as much information as possible regarding the work the student was expected to do throughout the course (criteria, due dates, etc.) and 3) information on the technological means to be used during the course.

Additionally, the satellite classes did not differ in the type of cognitive abilities required of the students during class: listening, reading, etc. But the broadcasting of the class did make a difference in certain respects: It was much easier to lose one's attention, and it was practically impossible to ask the professor to repeat something when a student did not understand or simply was not paying enough attention to what was said. By the time the professor received the request, he/she was already working on a different topic. Sudden transmission failures or interferences made this problem even more frequent. The problem was solved by videotaping the class, so that any student could review it at his/her own convenience and pace. However, this is certainly not the ideal solution.

Since 1992 all courses in our program have the self-study manuals that I have previously discussed. Their use has given us more time to concentrate on the feedback we give our students and has also allowed for more specific and content-related interaction outside and during the class sessions. All distance education programs are supported by various sorts of written materials that are produced. I believe that in our case the production of written materials by the faculty has been impressive: Three manuals during the first semester, and four during each of the following semesters. These materials have been re-edited every year. Students spend twelve hours weekly on each course, and the manuals guide their work from class to class (each class is broadcast every two weeks). This new instructional design clearly set our program apart from all others involved in SEIS, since our students were required to do much more study on their own, and the professor's role became more and more that of a guide and advisor, rather than a transmitter of information.

Since October 1994, we have been designing electronic, interactive, multimedia manuals. An example is the Sociolinguistics course, the second of the Applied Linguistics area courses. Producing multimedia manuals for all courses is an effort that will continue for the following years, not only in our master's program, but in all of the programs that are a part of SEIS. These cover a broad spectrum of levels including senior high school, undergraduate, and graduate courses. The technology needed for the use of these multimedia manuals will be available in each of the twenty-six campuses of the ITESM System by the time they are implemented as part of the course work. We believe that work with these manuals and their complementary written, audio, and video materials will take our students to yet a higher level of cognitive activity. We also hope that the new electronic manuals, given the possibilities they provide for student interaction with the content, self-paced learning, and student self-evaluation of their understanding of the materials, will allow us to further reduce the costly transmission time for each course. We hope to reduce time from one three-hour session every two weeks to a one-hour session of live interaction.

Interaction with Students via Electronic Mail Compared with Face-to-Face, Traditional Interaction. The off-line interaction that occurs through electronic mail has had three stages. From 1989 to 1990 some campuses could not make this technology accessible for all students. Even where it was available, it was not used because our faculty did not include off-line interaction as a required activity in their instructional design. In addition, electronic mail was new to most students and very few had an interest in struggling with computer interfaces if the phone was equally available. From 1990 to 1992 we used an electronic mail system called "Coordinator" that helped us send mainly academic administrative information to students. Some remote students used it as a channel for asking simple questions instead of using class time. Since 1992, we have been using two kinds of off-line communication: one, called QuickMail, mainly for administrative purposes and the other, called Pine, for communication between students and professors. An example of patterns of communication use is shown in Table 1.

Table 1. Student-Professor Interaction

Week of February 21 to March 1, 1995
for Course in the Education Area

	Face-to-Face	Telephone	Pine	QuickMail
Day 1	2	1	2	0
Day 2	1	3	3	0
Day 3	1	3	3	2
Day 4	3	6	3	1
Day 5	9	3	1	0
Day 6	0	2	3	0
Day 7	3	2	3	0
TOTAL	19	20	18	3

On-site students: 24/22 (91.6%) consulted the professor
Distant students: 82/38 (46.3%) consulted the professor

The evidence suggests that the on-site students are much more likely to seek the professors' advice than their distant peers (91.6% vs. 46.3%). Although on-site students have access to the interaction technology, it has been easier for them to visit the professor at her/his office. Distant students, on the other hand, seek advice either by phone or by e-mail. More orientation should be offered so students could benefit from the technology accessible to them.

Conclusions

We are convinced that the use of interactive satellite technology through the ITESM System has improved the educational quality in the following respects:

- Creating team work requirements that have encouraged interpersonal and interdisciplinary decisions among professors from different content areas and experts from the computer and communications areas.
- Optimizing the best professors, making their courses accessible to all students no matter where they study.
- By bringing students and professors from different regions together, both can focus on the relevant and significant aspects of the course, given the different regional contexts.
- Keeping the system flexible enough so that each course is free to adopt the educational model that best suits its needs has resulted in a diverse and unique distance education model.
- Class time interaction has been successful not only when it has been contemplated in the instructional design of the course or class but when it has been requested beforehand in the form of videos which students have to make and send to the transmitting site.

- Off-line interaction has proven less successful either because our students need more training in the use of computer networks or because of its accessibility.

Finally, I would like to close with a few remarks about our future development. The different electronic media described in this paper provide for an effective, though not ideal, teacher-student and student-student interaction. With our first steps into hypermedia technology, we are looking forward to studying in a more systematic way another important aspect of educational interaction: that of the student with the instructional materials.

Thus far, we have had little control over this dimension of interaction and little feedback from students as well. With our new hypermedia study guides, we hope to ensure a more interactive access to the materials, a faster feedback response, and, ultimately, encourage students toward a more independent and self-controlled learning process.

Notes:

1. The data in this portion of the paper are taken from the thesis research by Rosario Archila, a graduate of the program.

2. The three types of interaction were taken from a presentation by Charlotte N. Gunawardena at the 3rd Encuentro Intranacional de Educación a Distancia, Guadalajara, Mexico (November 1994).

Notes on Authors

Cheryl Achterberg is Associate Professor, Nutrition Department at The Pennsylvania State University. Address: 5 Henderson Building, Penn State Nutrition Center, University Park, PA 16802.

Zane L. Berge is Director, Training Systems at the University of Maryland Baltimore County-Department of Education. Address: ISD Graduate Program, 5401 Wilkens Avenue, Baltimore, MD 21228-5398.

Paul M. Biner is Professor, Department of Psychological Science at Ball State University. Address: Department of Psychological Science, Ball State University, Muncie, IN 47306.

Byron R. Burnham is Associate Dean, Learning Resources at Utah State University. Address: Learning Resources, UMC 3000, Utah State University, Logan, UT 84322-3000.

Lynn E. Davie is Professor at Ontario Institute for Studies in Education. Address: Ontario Institute for Studies in Education, 252 Bloor Street West, Toronto, Ontario, Canada M5S 1V6.

Margaret A. Koble is Publications Manager at The American Center for the Study of Distance Education, The Pennsylvania State University. Address: The Pennsylvania State University, 110 Rackley Building, University Park, PA 16802.

Allan C. Lauzon is Lecturer at the University of Guelph. Address: University of Guelph, Department of Rural Extension Studies, Ontario Agricultural College, Guelph, Ontario, Canada N1G 2W1.

Karen L. Murphy is Assistant Professor, Educational Curriculum and Instruction at Texas A & M University. Address: Educational Curriculum and Instruction, Mail Stop 4232, 308 Harrington Tower, College Station, TX 77843-4232.

Dora Esthela Rodríguez is Professor, I.T.E.S.M. Address: Ave. Eugenio Garza Sada, 2501 Sur Col. Technologico, Monterrey N.L., Mexico 64849.

Ellen D. Wagner is Vice President, Informania, Inc. Address: 444 DeHaro Street, Suite 128, San Francisco, CA 94107.

Available from ACSDE...

ACSDE RESEARCH MONOGRAPH   No. 15
The Effects of Distance Learning: Revised Edition

This monograph combines a review of literature with an annotated bibliography. It discusses issues relating to the effectiveness of distance education in a variety of contexts: K-12 and higher education, corporate and government settings, and the military.

≈ ≈ ≈ ≈ ≈ ≈ ≈ ≈

ACSDE RESEARCH MONOGRAPHS   Nos. 11–14
No. 11 *Distance Education Symposium 3: Policy and Administration*
No. 12 *Distance Education Symposium 3: Instruction*
No. 13 *Distance Education Symposium 3: Learners and Learning*
No. 14 *Distance Education Symposium 3: Course Design*

These monographs comprise selected papers presented at the Third Distance Education Research Symposium held at Penn State in May 1995. The articles focus on issues related to quality in distance education.

≈ ≈ ≈ ≈ ≈ ≈ ≈ ≈

ACSDE RESEARCH MONOGRAPH   No. 10
Internationalism in Distance Education: A Vision for Higher Education

These selected papers from the International Distance Education Conference held at Penn State in June 1994 discuss the techniques of successful international distance instruction, the challenges of administration, the development of policy, and the problems and potentials of accelerating exchanges between different cultures around the world.

≈ ≈ ≈ ≈ ≈ ≈ ≈ ≈

Forthcoming from ACSDE...

ACSDE RESEARCH MONOGRAPH   No. 16
Presence at a Distance: The Educator-Learner Relationship in Distance Education

≈ ≈ ≈ ≈ ≈ ≈ ≈ ≈

Also Available from ACSDE...

Readings in Distance Education Series
This series consists of articles selected from *The American Journal of Distance Education.* Each volume is a resource for teaching a particular aspect of the field of distance education.

No. 5 *K-12 Distance Education: Learning, Instruction, and Teacher Training*

Readings in Distance Education No. 5 consists of selected articles from *The Journal* that deal with K-12 distance education, including articles on learners and learning, instruction, teacher training, and administrative issues.

No. 4 *Video-based Telecommunications in Distance Education*
No. 3 *Distance Education for Corporate and Military Training*

For information contact:
The American Center for the Study of Distance Education
The Pennsylvania State University
110 Rackley Building
University Park, PA 16802-3202
Tel: (814) 863-3764   Fax: (814) 865-5878

2406

The American Journal of Distance Education

The American Journal of Distance Education is published by the American Center for the Study of Distance Education at The Pennsylvania State University. **The Journal** is designed for professional trainers; teachers in schools, colleges and universities; researchers; adult educators; and other specialists in education and communications. Created to disseminate information and act as a forum for criticism and debate about research in and the practice of distance education in the Americas, **The Journal** provides reports of new research, discussions of theory, and program developments in the field. **The Journal** is issued three times a year.

SELECTED CONTENTS

For information contact:
The American Journal of Distance Education
The Pennsylvania State University
110 Rackley Building
University Park, PA 16802-3202
Tel: (814) 863-3764   Fax: (814) 865-5878

Date Due

ILL			
4175497			
4/19/04			
ILL			
5503201			
7/1/05			